Pitman Chess Teaching Scheme

# Learn Chess

Edward Penn and John Littlewood

With contributions from Michael Basman, Bernard Cafferty,
Bill Hartston, John Nunn, Mike Price, John Roycroft

Pitman House

PITMAN HOUSE LIMITED
39 Parker Street, London WC2B 5PB

Associated Companies
Pitman Publishing Pty Ltd, Melbourne
Pitman Publishing New Zealand Ltd, Wellington

First published in Great Britain 1980

ISBN: 273  01237  1

Phototypeset in V.I.P. Century Schoolbook by
Western Printing Services Ltd, Bristol
Printed and bound in Great Britain
at The Pitman Press, Bath

# Contents

# Preface

## The Morgan Crucible Chess Tournament Series

Built into the Pitman Chess Teaching Scheme is a series of three Progress Tests, two in Stage One, a final Test in the next Stage and a series of tournaments restricted to successful candidates. The Scheme, sponsored by Morgan Crucibles, involves a Progress Test after Unit 14 (Student's Book – Stage 1) a second-level Test after Unit 30, and a top level Test at the end of the next Stage for those who wish to continue the scheme to that point (full details obtainable from the publisher). A bronze badge and a certificate will be awarded to each successful student in the third-level Test, a silver badge and certificate for success in the second-level Test, and a gold badge and certificate in the top level Test.

The first of the Morgan Crucible Chess Tournament Series will be held in 1981, and be open to teams of five, plus one reserve, which have obtained a pass in the third-level Progress Test. The early rounds will be held at local level, then regional and zonal levels, and then the last eight teams be invited to London at the sponsor's expense to play the Quarter-finals, Semi-finals and Finals.

\*       \*       \*

"The Morgan Crucible Company is glad to be associated with an innovation in the teaching of chess and is sponsoring a series of chess tournaments based on the Pitman Chess Teaching Scheme.

I commend the Scheme to teachers, in the hope that pupils will learn a leisure activity of lasting and worthwhile value."

I. Weston Smith
Chairman

# Introduction

This introduction is brief but very important. It is brief because few
people read long introductions and you really should read this one in
order to gain the greatest benefit from the Pitman Chess Teaching
Scheme (PCTS).

Chess is a game that will give you a great deal of enjoyment if you
learn to play it properly.

As the different pieces are able to move in different ways it may at
first seem that chess is a difficult game to learn, but you will soon
remember the basic moves and be able to set up the board and play.
You will certainly enjoy these early games and should play as often as
possible, against anyone who will give you a game. Of course you will
make mistakes – some of which you will get away with, others you will
not – and you will lose many games, probably more than you will win,
but this is only to be expected. You will, however, enjoy the game more
and become a better player more quickly if you study the lessons in the
Pitman Chess Teaching Scheme properly.

To make chess easier to learn, the game is divided into three main
parts – the opening, the middle game and the end game.

THE OPENING is concerned with developing (moving) your pieces to the
best available squares depending upon the kind of game you wish to
play.

THE MIDDLE GAME usually involves a mixture of planning and of
exchanging pieces, while trying to obtain the best position for yourself.

THE END GAME, where there are usually just a few pieces and
sometimes only Kings and pawns remaining, is when you try to force a
win – unless, of course, you have already checkmated (and therefore
beaten) your opponent, or he has resigned (given you the game) because
you had more pieces, or were in a much better position after the
exchanges in the opening and/or middle game.

You will need to learn the rules and the principles that apply to each of these three parts, but remember that the game is divided only to make it easier to discuss. Chess is really one complete game and every single move is important.

To enable us to discuss any one of the sixty-four squares on the chessboard, each square is given a letter and a number. This is called algebraic notation. You may come across other types of notation, notably English descriptive, but since most beginners find algebraic notation easier it has been used throughout this book.

We start by teaching you to play some simple end games accurately. After all, you do not want to play a game well only to lose it because you did not understand the correct way to make the final, and very important, moves.

End games are great fun. You can set one up and play it through to a finish in a few moves, and the principles you learn while doing so will help your whole game to improve and will give you confidence. When you know you are a good end-game player, you play more sensibly and safely in the middle game; you get to know the sort of end-game positions from which you can win, and this encourages you to aim for these better positions earlier on. This in turn helps you to decide upon the type of opening you should play, and the net result is that you play the whole game better and enjoy it all the more – and you begin to win more often too!

If and when you play for your club or school, or start entering chess tournaments yourself, you will meet players who have learned to play the game properly. If you have learned to play it properly too, then you need fear no-one. Even if you do not win, you will know that you played the game well and that the player who beat you had to play very well to do so.

It is up to you to study the lessons properly and to learn them well. Remember what you learn. If you are in doubt, try to find the answer yourself before referring to the book again. Play and practise as often as possible. No matter what help you may get from other sources it will depend largely upon your own efforts how soon you become a good player. Above all enjoy yourself!

## Laws, Rules and Principles

Even experienced players can be confused by these three terms, so it is better that they are explained now, before you meet them in the text of this book.

LAWS of chess are officially made and kept up to date by a group of international chess experts, who make up an organization known (in French) as the Fédération Internationale des Échecs. This title is nearly always shortened to its initials and is known as FIDÉ (pronounced 'feeday'). The laws cover everything from the moves of the game to the international rating of players' strengths and when, where and how international tournaments are to be played. There can be no argument against the laws – they are final and binding.

RULES are not binding but are intended to be a guide to the playing of the game itself. They have been developed over many years from the experience gained in millions of games, and while they are often useful, there are times when it is best to go against them. Choosing the right time to ignore a rule is one of the keys to success in chess. As you play more chess you will hear and read 'rules' that say *always* do this' and '*never* do that', but there are often exceptions to these in chess; nothing is 'always' or 'never' – just 'usually' or 'as a rule'!

PRINCIPLES are the 'best ideas' of chess. The principles of end-game play, for example, refer to the best way of playing certain types of positions – the best ideas behind certain moves or series of moves. You would seldom go against what you know to be the principles involved in a certain situation, and a sound knowledge of principles in chess, particularly in end-game play, is essential for success at any level of the game.

# Unit 1

Chess is a game played between two people. They begin the game with 16 chessmen each and play on a board made up of 64 squares.

## The Chessboard

The squares of the chessboard are arranged in eight rows of eight and are alternately coloured dark and light. Many different materials and colours are used in the manufacture of chessboards, but to make it easier to talk about the game the squares are always called *black* and *white*, regardless of their actual colour.

The players face each other from opposite ends of the board, which is placed so the right-hand corner square nearest each player is white ('white on the right'), as shown in diagram 1.1 (above, centre).

In diagram 1.2 (centre, below) the rows running across the board are numbered '1' to '8', while the rows running from top to bottom of the board are lettered 'a' to 'h'. The former are called RANKS, the latter FILES.

Note that when naming the squares lower case letters: abcdefgh

are used. This is because capital letters are used to denote pieces.

Black

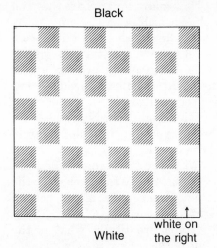

White    white on the right

*Diagram 1.1*

Every file is known by a letter and every rank by a number, so by using a letter and a number together we can pinpoint any one of the 64 squares on the board.

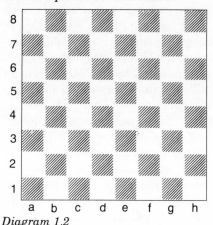

*Diagram 1.2*
*The files on a chessboard are known by letters, and the ranks by numbers.*

In diagram 1.3 (below, centre) for example, you will see that there is a cross in one of the white squares. By looking first at which file the square is on (in this case the e-file) and then which rank (number 4) you will see that this square is called e4.

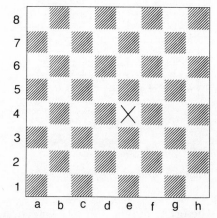

*Diagram 1.3*

*The chessboard. The players face each other, and the board is placed so that there is a white corner square to the right of each player.*

In diagram 1.4 (below) the file letter and rank number are shown for every square. This system of notation is called ALGEBRAIC NOTATION.

Practise pinpointing certain squares on your own board and naming them as quickly as you can. This is best done with another player, sitting at the opposite end of the board, who can point to a square while you name it. After a while, you point to certain squares and let

Black

| | a | b | c | d | e | f | g | h | |
|---|---|---|---|---|---|---|---|---|---|
| 8 | a8 | b8 | c8 | d8 | e8 | f8 | g8 | h8 | 8 |
| 7 | a7 | b7 | c7 | d7 | e7 | f7 | g7 | h7 | 7 |
| 6 | a6 | b6 | c6 | d6 | e6 | f6 | g6 | h6 | 6 |
| 5 | a5 | b5 | c5 | d5 | e5 | f5 | g5 | h5 | 5 |
| 4 | a4 | b4 | c4 | d4 | e4 | f4 | g4 | h4 | 4 |
| 3 | a3 | b3 | c3 | d3 | e3 | f3 | g3 | h3 | 3 |
| 2 | a2 | b2 | c2 | d2 | e2 | f2 | f2 | h2 | 2 |
| 1 | a1 | b1 | c1 | d1 | e1 | f1 | g1 | h1 | 1 |
| | a | b | c | d | e | f | g | h | |

White

*Diagram 1.4*

*How the squares are named.*

the other player name them. Then change ends and repeat the exercise. This is important, since the player who will have the white pieces always sits with the 'a' file on his left, while the player who will have the black pieces always has the 'a' file on his right.

So although the actual names of the squares remain the same, the squares themselves seem to be in a different part of the board, depending upon whether you are sitting at Black's end or White's. If you are Black, the white square a8 will be in your bottom right-hand corner; while if you are White, it will be in your top left.

## Questions on Unit 1

1   How many squares are there on a chessboard?
2   How many chessmen does each player have at the start of a game?
3   The numbered rows run across the board, from side to side. What are they called?
4   What eight letters are used for the rows running from top to bottom of the board?
5   What are these rows called?
6   If you are White, what is the name of the square in your bottom right-hand corner?
7   If you are Black, what is the name of the square in your top left-hand corner?
8   What colour is the square in Black's bottom left-hand corner?

*          *          *

There are many different stories about how chess originated. One of them, interesting but almost certainly not true, states that the game was invented around 500 B.C. by an Indian named Sassa. He intended the game to represent a battle between two armies, and his Rajah was so pleased with it that he offered Sassa a reward.

The wily Sassa asked for a quantity of corn: one grain to be placed on the first square of the board, two grains on the second, four on the third, and so on. But this was an impossible request. Long before

reaching the 64th square there would be far too many grains to fit on a chessboard square of any size. Indeed, doubling the number in this way would result in more than eighteen million million million grains!

*          *          *

## Answers to Questions on Unit 1

| 1 | 64. | 5 | Files. |
|---|---|---|---|
| 2 | 16. | 6 | hl. |
| 3 | Ranks. | 7 | hl. |
| 4 | a b c d e f g h. | 8 | Black. |

# Unit 2

## The Pieces

Chessmen, like chessboards, are manufactured from many different materials and colours, but to make it easier to talk about them they are always called *black* and *white*. Each player starts the game with an army of 16 chessmen – 1 King, 1 Queen, 2 Bishops, 2 Knights, 2 Rooks and 8 pawns.

The type of chess set normally used is called a Staunton pattern set. It is based upon a set designed in the mid-nineteenth century and named after Howard Staunton, a leading English player of the time.

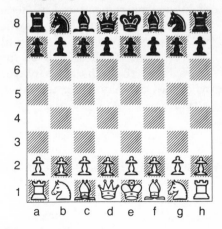

*Diagram 2.1*

When chess diagrams are printed, symbols are used to represent the various pieces. Diagram 2.1 shows a set ready for play, using the symbols representing the pieces shown in the photograph of the Staunton pattern set above.

The following tips will help you to remember how to set up the pieces ready for play.

1.  White *always* has the a-file on his left.
2.  Whichever colour you are playing there is *always* a white square in the bottom right-hand corner of the board – h1 if you have the white pieces, a8 if you have the black.
3.  The Queens are placed on the d-file – the white Queen on a white square (d1) and the black Queen on a black square (d8).

The half of the board made up of files a, b, c and d is called the QUEEN'S SIDE. It remains the Queen's side throughout the game, regardless of where the Queens may be moved during play. The other half of the board (files e, f, g and h) is called the KING'S SIDE.

Chess diagrams are usually shown with the black pieces at the top and the white pieces at the bottom. This means that when you are playing through games and exercises using diagrams White is playing *up* the board and Black is playing *down*.

To ensure that you understand exactly which symbol represents which piece, look at the accompanying sketch. This shows the name, the Staunton pattern piece, the symbol and an initial that represents each of the chessmen. The initial only is used in notation, rather than writing the name of the piece in full. Note that the letter 'N' is used to represent the Knight. This is because 'K' is used for the King.

White *always* has the opening move in any chess game. Black replies, and the players continue to move alternately thereafter. Only one piece at a time may be moved, except when *castling* – which is described in Unit 13 – but you need not worry about castling until you have learned the moves of the individual pieces.

Each piece is moved in a different way, but these basic moves are not difficult to remember. In fact it will probably take less time for you to learn the moves than it takes to explain them!

## Questions on Unit 2

1  On what square does the black King start the game?
2  Which files make up the Queen's side of the board?
3  From a position in a diagram, should White be playing up or down the board?
4  What initial represents the Knight in notation?
5  What pieces stand in the corner squares at the start of the game?
6  How many pawns does each player have at the start of a game?

\*     \*     \*

As long ago as 1749 a leading French chess player, Francois-Andre Danican Philidor, wrote a book entitled *Analyse du jeu des Eschecs* ('Analysis of the Game of Chess'). In this he stressed the importance of pawns. Indeed, he said 'pawns are the *soul* of chess'.

Considering that Philidor pointed this out so long ago it is amazing how many experienced chess players still 'throw away' pawns as though they have no value. In the next Unit, as you learn about pawns remember Philidor's words. Always treat your pawns with respect, and your eventual improvement in chess will be far more rapid than that of a player who does not pay them too much attention.

\*     \*     \*

| K | Q | N | B | R |
| King | Queen | Knight | Bishop | Rook |

## Answers to questions on Unit 2

| 1 | e8. | 4 | N. |
| 2 | a, b, c, d. | 5 | Rooks. |
| 3 | Up. | 6 | 8. |

# Unit 3

## The Pawn

Each pawn moves in a straight line along the file upon which it starts the game, provided that the square immediately in front of it is clear, i.e. not occupied by any other piece. A pawn *cannot* jump over other pieces, either its own or the enemy's (as in draughts or checkers).

On its first move it can move either one *or* two squares forward, but after its first move it can only move forward one square at a time. This applies to all eight pawns of both sides. It does not matter how many moves have already been made by other pawns or pieces, each pawn still has the choice of moving forward one or two squares *on its first move*.

Pawns *never* move backwards.

The only time a pawn can move off the file upon which it started the game is when it captures an enemy piece. Pawns capture diagonally one square forward, removing the enemy piece from the board and taking its place.

You are not forced to make a capture, even if an enemy piece is standing on a square your pawn is controlling.

Set up diagrams 3.1, 3.2 and 3.3 one at a time and practise the moves described.

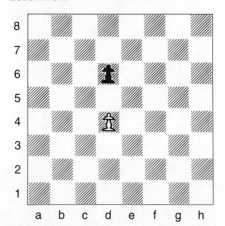

*Diagram 3.1   Black's pawn on d6 could capture any enemy piece that moved onto either c5 or e5. Black's pawn could be said to be 'controlling' these two squares. White is also 'controlling' c5 and e5 with his pawn on d4, and it depends upon who is to move whether the pawns can be thought of as attacking or defending these two squares. This is why we use the word 'control'.*

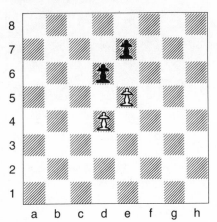

*Diagram 3.2   Here White's e-pawn and Black's d-pawn could each capture the other, depending upon whose turn it was to move, but in both cases the opponent could recapture. If, for instance, White captured Black's pawn on d6, the pawn on e7 could recapture. Similarly, if Black captured the white pawn on e5, the pawn on d4 could recapture. Instead of capturing, each side could move either of their pawns one square forward. From the diagram position Black would not be able to move his pawn on e7 two squares forward – even though it would be that pawn's first move – because e5 is occupied.*

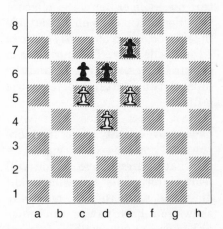

*Diagram 3.3   Here we can see how pawns fight like foot-soldiers. If we imagine that each has a shield held in front of him we can understand why he is safe from a direct attack from another foot-soldier. (You will learn later that other pieces are much more powerful and against them this shield is no defence). But another foot-soldier can thrust his sword diagonally forward (around his shield) and attack an oppo-*

*nent. This is a useful way to remember how a pawn captures.*

*In this diagram, both sides' c-pawns are safe from each other, but White's pawn on c5 could be captured by Black's d-pawn. If Black did make this capture, White would be able to recapture with his pawn on d4 – if he wanted to, of course. If it were White to move, he would have a definite advantage because he is attacking Black's d-pawn twice (from c5 and e5), while it is defended only once (by the pawn on e7). In this case, White could win a pawn.*

The pawns of files *b* to *g* can capture pieces on either of the adjacent two files, but pawns on the outside files, *a* and *h*, can obviously capture on one side only. The a-pawn can capture pieces on the b-file and the h-pawn can capture pieces on the g-file.

Most chess games start with pawn moves. (Only one of the more powerful pieces could make an alternative first move as you will learn later.) The following eight diagrams, while they are mainly to show you how pawns can move either one or two squares forward on their first move, will give you a brief introduction to some of the openings that you will come across later. Practise them on your own board.

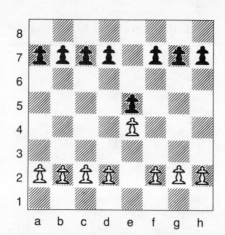

*Diagram 3.4 White has opened the game by moving his e-pawn forward two squares, from e2 to e4. Black's reply, e7 to e5, also takes advantage of the fact that a pawn can move two squares forward on its first move. Many chess games open like this.*

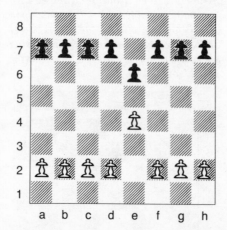

*Diagram 3.5 Again White opens with e2–e4, but this time Black is content with moving his e-pawn only one square forward, to e6.*

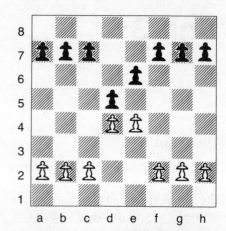

*Diagram 3.6 Following the opening moves in diag. 3.4, White has played d2–d4 as his second move, and Black has replied d7–d5. This opening is known as the 'French Defence'.*

*Because pawns capture diagonally one square forward, White can now – if he chooses – capture Black's pawn on d5 with his own pawn on e4. See diag. 3.7.*

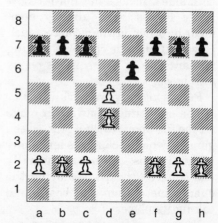

*Diagram 3.7 White has made the capture on d5, but now Black can recapture with his pawn on e6. See diag. 3.8.*

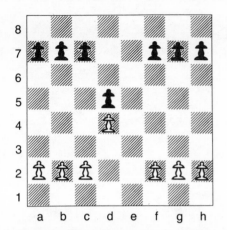

Diagram 3.8 *Now both sides have played three moves and each has captured a pawn. They have 'exchanged' pawns. This is known as the 'Exchange Variation of the French Defence'. Diag. 3.9 shows another variation after the position shown in diag. 3.6.*

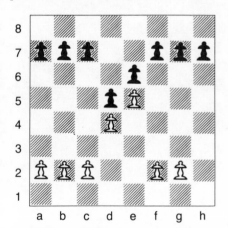

Diagram 3.9 *As you know, you are not forced to make a capture, even if it is possible to do so. Here, from the position shown in diag. 3.6, White has chosen to move his e-pawn on from e4 to e5 instead of capturing on d5. This is known as the* 'Nimzovitch Variation of the French Defence' *after Aaron Nimzovitch (1886–1935), who was one of the greatest chess 'thinkers' the game has known.*

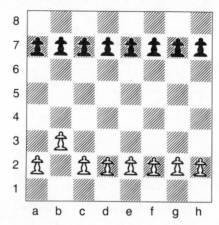

Diagram 3.10 *White usually takes advantage of being able to move two squares forward with one of his pawns (most often the d- or e-pawn) to open a game, but in some openings he moves only one square. An example is 1 b2–b3, known as 'Larsen's Opening' after another of the world's top chess players, Danish Grand Master Bent Larsen.*

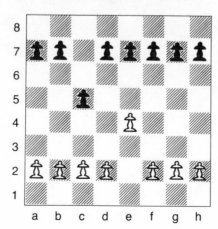

Diagram 3.11 *A very popular opening, known as the 'Sicilian Defence', begins when Black replies to 1 e2–e4 by playing 1 . . . c7–c5.*
*After these opening moves there are many variations for both sides.*

## Questions on Unit 3

1 Can a pawn capture an enemy piece on a square immediately in front of itself on the same file?
2 When can a pawn move off the file upon which it starts the game?
3 When can a pawn move backwards?
4 Can a pawn ever move more than one square forward?
5 If you have answered 'yes' to Question 4, *when* can a pawn move more than one square forward in one move?
6 On which file or files can the e-pawn capture?
7 On which file or files can the h-pawn capture?
8 Can a pawn jump over other pieces?

\* \* \*

The pawn did not always have the choice of moving either one or two squares forward on its first move.

For almost 1,000 years there had been no significant change in the game, when in the fifteenth century it reached Italy, and the Italians – no doubt inspired by the Renaissance – sought to make some refreshing changes.

This they did by giving more power to some of the pieces, which, added to the extra privilege they gave to the pawns, allowed the two sides to get to grips much more quickly. It led to earlier fighting for control of the central squares, and the pieces were able to get into action in fewer moves than had previously been necessary.

\*       \*       \*

## Answers to Questions on Unit 3

| | | | |
|---|---|---|---|
| 1 | No. | 5 | On its first move only. |
| 2 | When it makes a capture. | 6 | d and f. |
| 3 | Never. | 7 | g. |
| 4 | Yes. | 8 | No. |

# Unit 4

## Capturing 'en passant'

*En passant* is a French expression which means 'in passing' and applies *only* to pawns and *only* in the following circumstances.

If you move any pawn two squares forward on its first move and in doing so it passes over a square that is controlled by an enemy *pawn*, your pawn can be captured 'en passant' – as though it had, in fact, moved only one square. An example of this is shown in diag. 4.1.

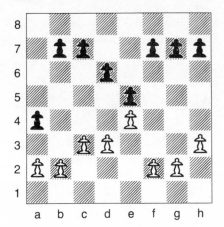

*Diagram 4.1    Let us say that from this position it is White to play and he decides to move his pawn from b2 to b4. It may*

seem that by doing so he will avoid the possibility of being captured by Black's pawn on a4, which is controlling b3.

But the white pawn does not avoid the possibility of capture. Black can, if he wishes, capture this white pawn by moving his pawn from a4 to b3 and removing the white pawn from b4 – though White had only moved one square forward.

This is capturing 'en passant'.

The possibility of moving a pawn two squares forward on its first move was introduced only to speed up the game and not to allow any pawn to avoid an attacked square in this way.

If your opponent *does* choose to capture en passant he *must* do so on his very next move. He cannot do it later.

Just to be sure that this slightly unusual move is firmly fixed in your mind, set up on your board the position in diagram 4.2. This gives you another example of an en passant capture, but this time at Black's end of the board.

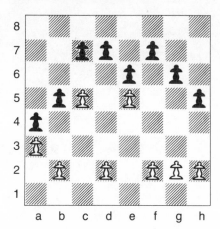

*Diagram 4.2    If Black were to move his pawn from d7 to d5, White could capture it en passant either by moving his pawn from c5 to d6 or by moving his pawn from e5 to d6.*

*If Black chose to move his pawn from f7 to f5, White could capture en passant by moving his pawn from e5 to f6.*

*In each case the enemy pawn is, of course, removed from the board.*

Always remember – it is ONLY PAWNS that can capture or be captured en passant.

## Questions on Unit 4

1 Look at diag. 4.1. If White moved his pawn from f2 to f4, could this pawn be captured en passant?
2 Again in diag. 4.1, if Black moved his pawn from a4 to a3, could White capture this pawn en passant?
3 What does 'en passant' mean?
4 If the opportunity presents itself, are you *forced* to capture en passant?
5 If you do have a chance to capture en passant, can you wait a few moves before making the capture?
6 Can any piece make an en passant capture?

\*     \*     \*

Capturing *en passant* was a natural result of giving the pawn the option of moving two squares on its first move.

The players naturally began to

exploit the possibility of waiting for an opponent to get a pawn on the fifth rank and then, by moving one of their own pawns on an adjacent file two squares forward, avoiding the square controlled by the enemy pawn. This obviously worked against the idea of speeding up the game, so the en passant capture was introduced.

Another change in the game introduced during the Renaissance was the facility of promoting a pawn when it reached the eighth rank. As pawns cannot move backwards, once one reached the enemy's back rank it could go no further, and allowing it to be promoted to a more powerful piece made the game far more interesting and the pawn itself a great deal more valuable.

*    *    *

## Answers to Questions on Unit 4

1 No. Black could capture White's f-pawn with his e-pawn, but this is a normal capture – *not* an en passant capture.

2 No. White's b-pawn could make a normal capture.

3 In passing.

4 No.

5 No. En passant captures *must* be made on the very next move.

6 No. Only pawns can capture or be captured en passant.

# Unit 5

## Pawn Promotion

If you get a pawn through to your opponent's back rank it earns promotion. You may promote it to any piece except a King – even though you may still have other pieces on the board. It cannot remain a pawn because, since pawns move forwards (*never* backwards or directly sideways), once it reaches the back rank it can go no further.

You *must* announce to what piece you are promoting your pawn *before* your opponent plays his next move. Indeed, your own move is *not complete* until you have stated the new value of your promoted pawn and have replaced it with the appropriate piece. See diagrams 5.1 and 5.2.

It is usual to promote to a Queen because, as you will learn later, the Queen is normally the most powerful piece on the board. You can promote to a Queen even if you still have your original Queen on the board. It is virtually impossible to promote all eight pawns, but if you did so you could promote them to Queens, Rooks, Bishops, Knights, or any mixture of these pieces, regardless of whatever pieces you may still have on the board.

Promoting is often called 'queening' because it is usual to promote to a Queen, but there will be times when it will suit you better to promote to a Rook, a Bishop or a Knight. The reasons for this will be explained later.

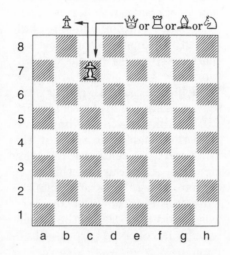

Diagram 5.1 Promoting a pawn. Let us suppose that White moves his pawn to c8. He must now promote it by removing from the board and replacing it with an appropriate piece.

If White decided to promote to a Queen and a spare Queen were not available, he could use a Rook turned upside-down to represent his new Queen.

Another way to represent an extra Queen is to use two pawns on the same square.

Pawns can be promoted when they reach the back rank on any file.

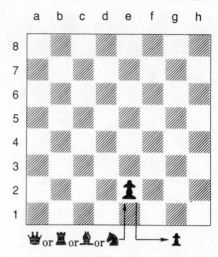

Diagram 5.2 Black promotes a pawn by playing from e2 to e1.

Remember that in chess diagrams White plays up the board and Black plays down the board.

Many beginners (and even some experienced players) do not attach enough importance to their pawns. Probably because there are eight of them to start with, pawns are often given away or moved carelessly. You should always take great care of your pawns and consider their moves carefully, since once you have moved a pawn you can *never* move it back again. Because pawns can earn promotion they are obviously very valuable, but they play an important part in a game whether or not they eventually gain promotion. Treat them with respect.

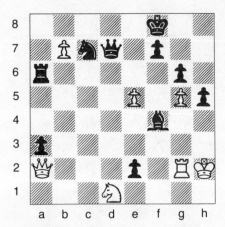

*Diagram 5.3.*

## Questions on Unit 5

1   Look at diag. 5.3. If Black moved his e-pawn from e2 to e1, could he promote it to a Queen?

2   With the same move, could Black promote the pawn to a Bishop?

3   Could Black capture the Knight on d1?

4   Would he still be able to promote the pawn if he did capture the Knight?

5   Could White promote a pawn on his next move from the diagram position?

6   If a player gets a pawn onto his opponent's back rank, does it have to be promoted or can it remain a pawn?

\*　　\*　　\*

It is generally thought that chess originated in north-west India as a game called 'chaturanga', sometime around the sixth century A.D. The players called the most important piece the 'Rajah'. When the game was taken up in Persia, later in that century, this piece became known as the 'Shah'. The expression 'checkmate' was derived from 'Shah mat', which means 'the Shah is dead'. The name of the game was shortened by the Persians to 'chatrang'.

During the seventh century A.D. the Arabs started to play 'chatrang', still calling the most important piece the 'Shah'. But when, in the ninth and tenth centuries, the game moved on into Europe, this piece became generally known as the King. In Russia, however, the King was – and still is – called the 'Korol', which is derived from Charlemagne, who was also called Carolus Magnus (or Charles the Great).

\*　　\*　　\*

## Answers to Questions on Unit 5

1   Yes. Although Black still has his original Queen, he could promote the pawn to another Queen.

2   Yes. Or he could promote it to a Rook or a Knight instead.

3   Yes. Since pawns capture diagonally one square forward, the white Knight on d1 could be captured by Black's e-pawn in this position.

4   Yes. Once a pawn reaches the enemy's back rank, either by a final direct move or when making a capture, it has to be promoted.

5   Yes. White could move his b-pawn from b7 to b8 and earn promotion.

6   Once a pawn reaches the enemy's back rank, it *must* be promoted.

# Unit 6

## The King

The King is the most important piece in your chess army, even though his moves may seem to be rather limited.

Like the pawn, the King can move only one square at a time; but unlike the pawn, he can move in any direction – provided that the square he wishes to move to is not occupied by one of his own pieces, or is not being attacked by an enemy piece. If an enemy piece occupies the square to which the King wants to move, the King can, if he wishes, capture the enemy piece – provided that it is not being protected by another piece. The captured piece is then removed from the board.

The King himself can never be captured and removed from the board, since the game is lost when he is attacked by an enemy piece or pieces and cannot escape. When the King is being attacked he is said to be 'in check', and if he cannot escape he is said to be 'checkmated'.

If your King is placed in check you *must* do something about it immediately, since it is illegal to move any other piece while your king is in check.

There are three ways you can get your King out of check:
i by moving the King, where possible, to a square that is not directly attacked by an enemy piece;
ii by capturing the attacking piece – either with your King or with any other piece – provided that such a move is legally possible;
iii by placing a piece between your King and the attacking piece (interposing) – again provided that such a move is legally possible.

Obviously if the King was attacked by a pawn, interposing would be impossible since there can be no empty squares between the attacking pawn and the King. Pawns attack diagonally one square forward, so the attacking pawn must be on a square adjoining that occupied by the King.

When you learn the moves of the other pieces, however, you will see that they can attack from greater distances and that there will often be a number of empty squares between the King and the attacking piece. In these cases, interposing might of course be possible.

Diagrams 6.1 to 6.7 will help you to understand the things a King can and cannot do.

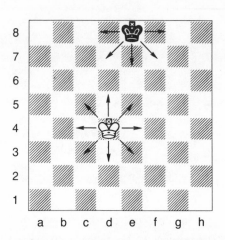

*Diagram 6.1 The maximum number of squares that a King could move to is eight.*

*If he was at the edge of the board, he could only move to one of five squares, while if he was in a corner only three squares at most would be open to him.*

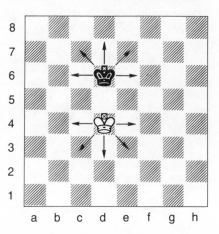

*Diagram 6.2 Although there are eight unoccupied squares within reach of each King, neither King could move to c5, d5 or e5, since Kings can never occupy adjoining squares.*

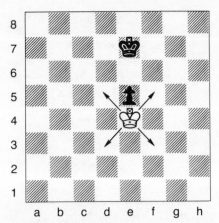

*Diagram 6.3 Here the white King could move to any one of six squares. He could capture Black's pawn on e5, or he could move to d5, f5, d3, e3 or f3. He could not move to d4 or f4, since Black's pawn is controlling these squares and the white King would be moving into check, which is illegal.*

*Black's King could move to any one of the eight squares around him.*

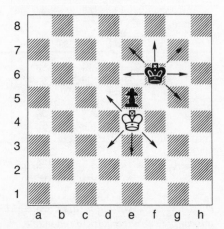

*Diagram 6.4 The black King is now protecting his pawn, so White cannot capture it nor can White move his King*

*to f5. Either move would place him on a square adjoining that of the black King.*

*The black pawn still controls d4 and f4, so White could only move to one of four squares from the diagram position – d3, e3, f3 and d5.*

## Stalemate

Stalemate occurs when your King is not in check but cannot move without moving into check and you cannot move any other piece instead.

There are many ways you can fall into the stalemate trap, and diag. 6.5 shows one of these.

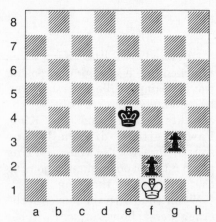

*Diagram 6.5 Black has two pawns, White has none. With correct play Black must be able to promote one of his pawns and win easily, regardless of whose turn it is to move from the diagram position. Unless . . . .*

If, in diag. 6.5, it were Black to play and he moved his King to f3,

White, although he has only a King against a King and two pawns, would get away with a draw – because he would be stalemated.

Black would be kicking himself, and well he should, for allowing White to get off the hook. He should have seen that White cannot move to e1 or g1 because those squares are controlled by the black pawn on f2. Since this pawn is protected by the pawn on g3, the white King cannot capture it.

So White has the possibility of only two legal moves – to e2 or g2 – and if Black did move his King to f3 he would deny the white King even these. (Kings cannot occupy adjoining squares.) So stalemate – a draw.

Watch out for this sort of thing in play. You can think that you are winning easily – as you would be if you were Black in diag. 6.5 – and then, one careless move and the win becomes a sad draw.

The simplest way for Black to end the game successfully is for him to move his King to e3 or d3, so that the white King cannot move to e2. White is forced to move to g2 instead, and there is now nothing to stop Black moving his King to e2, thereby gaining control of the 'Queening' square, f1. Now it does not matter where White moves. Black can even afford to let him capture the pawn on g3, since Black will promote his f-pawn next move – on f1 – and White can do nothing at all about it.

Play this ending through on your own board, since it is important that you should grasp the essentials of stalemate as soon as possible.

By now you could be thinking that the King is more of a liability to you than an asset. Certainly in the early and middle stages of a game it is usually wise to keep him safely tucked away while your other pieces do the fighting. But in the end game it is a different story. The King becomes very much a fighting piece himself and the way you use him, together with any other pieces you may have left, is often what decides the result.

## Questions on Unit 6

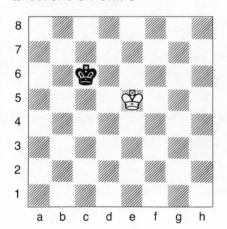

*Diagram 6.6*

1   As you know the King can move one square at a time in any direction. In diagram 6.6 are there any squares to which neither King can move? If so, name them.

2   The white King in diagram 6.7 can move to e4, e6, f5 and f6. Why can he *not* move to f4?

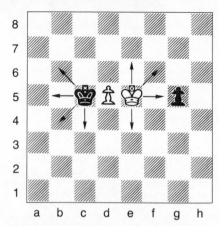

*Diagram 6.7*

3   Can the white King capture the black pawn?
4   Can the black King capture the white pawn?
5   No diagram this time, but imagine a position where it is your move, your King is *not* in check but cannot move without moving *into* check, and you cannot move any other piece. Have you lost the game?
6   Can a King capture an unprotected enemy piece, whether or not that piece is giving check?

\*      \*      \*

In Unit 1 'algebraic notation' was mentioned as one way of writing down the moves of a chess game. Before you start on the exercises in Unit 8, and throughout the rest of this book, you will need to know more about this system. Unit 7 contains all you need to know for now, so study it well before you go on to the remaining Units.

Another form of notation is known as 'English Descriptive' in which the capital letters of the pieces are, of course, the same as in algebraic but the squares are numbered differently. Algebraic notation is the style used in the Pitman Chess Teaching Scheme but in Unit 7 we also give brief details of English Descriptive notation so you will be able to follow chess books using that style.

You will quickly get used to chess notation but should write down as many of your games as possible in order to practise it. Writing down your games is also an excellent way of measuring your own progress. You can go over a game you have played and find out where you, or your opponent, made a particularly good or bad move, and it is great fun to play through some of your games weeks, months, even years after you played them and see how much you have improved.

\*      \*      \*

## Answers to Questions on Unit 6

1 Diagram 6.6 There are two squares to which neither King can move – d5 and d6 – because this would mean their occupying adjoining squares, which is illegal.

2 Diagram 6.7 The white King cannot move to f4, since he would be moving into check from Black's pawn on g5. (Remember Black is playing *down* the board in diagrams.)

3 Diagram 6.7 No. The black pawn is two squares away and the King can move only one square at a time.

4 Diagram 6.7 No. The white pawn is protected by his King. Otherwise the black King could make the capture, since the pawn is only one square away.

5 No. The game is drawn because it is stalemate.

6 Yes, provided that the piece is on an adjoining square.

# Unit 7

## Chess Notation

You already know that in algebraic notation each square on the chessboard is referred to by a letter and a number, and that *small* letters are always used to define the files –

a b c d e f g h

– since *capital* letters are used to identify the pieces –

K Q R B N

Although we have only considered King and pawn moves up to now, we really need to use one of the other pieces as well to demonstrate how to use algebraic notation, and the easiest piece we can choose for this purpose is the Bishop.

The Bishop is dealt with more fully in Unit 10, but for now it is enough to tell you that this piece always moves diagonally on squares of the same colour.

If, for example, we move White's King's Bishop from his starting square (f1) to b5, we simply write –

Bb5

A capture is shown by a small 'x', so if our Bishop made a capture on b5, we would write the move as –

Bxb5

If our move places the enemy King in check, we put a plus sign after the move –

Bxb5+

When a pawn is moved we only name the square to which it moves, since we do not use a capital letter to identify this piece. But if we make a capture with a pawn we put the letter of the file from which the pawn moved, then the 'takes' sign (x) and finally the square upon which the pawn makes the capture. For example, if a black pawn on a7 captured a white pawn on b6, we would write –

. . . axb6

The dots before this move tell us that it was Black's move; had we wished to show White's move we would have written it where the dots are. This idea is always used in chess notation.

If a pawn capture is made en passant we put the small letters 'ep' after the move, although this is not done in all books. The writing of 'ep' after an en passant capture is optional but we think it is best shown. Note that when writing down an en passant capture, the square to which the capturing pawn actually moves is given and *not* the square from which the enemy pawn is taken.

Sometimes in chess notation a move is immediately followed by a question mark ? or an exclamation mark !. A question mark means that the move was 'bad'; two question marks that it was 'terribly bad' – a 'blunder'. An exclamation mark means that the move was 'good'; two exclamation marks that it was 'brilliant'.

When a pawn is promoted we note the actual pawn move. For example, if a white pawn moved from f7 to f8 it would have reached the opponents's back rank and would have to be promoted, let us presume to a Queen. Here we could write –

f8=Q

Obviously we could have promoted to a Rook, a Bishop or a Knight, in which case our move would read –

f8=R, f8=B or f8=N

If the new piece gives check immediately to the King, we would write (for example)

f8=Q+

Rooks move in a straight line across a rank or up and down a file. If both Rooks were on the same *rank* with no other pieces between them and we want to show which one of the Rooks is moved, we name the *file* from which it moves. Suppose we have a Rook on a1 and the other on h1 and we want to move the Rook from the a-file, we would write –

Rae1

If both Rooks were on the same *file*, we then give the *rank* from which we move a Rook. So if we have a Rook on g2 and the other on g8 and we wish to move the Rook from g2 to g4, we would write –

R2g4

The possibility of either of one

player's two identical pieces being able to move to the same square could also happen with Knights.

Chess notation may seem a little difficult to understand at first but don't worry about it. It is, in fact, quite simple, and with practice you will soon find it very easy to use. It is essential that you learn chess notation as without it you could not record your own games or understand the move sequences given in books.

In 'figurine' algebraic notation the piece concerned in the move (except the pawn) are shown by their symbol. You would not attempt to sketch these symbols when writing down the moves yourself, but you would use the initials of the pieces.

For example, the move normally shown as –

   ♗xb5

you would write as –

   Bxb5+

In other languages the pieces are known by different names and consequently the initials are sometimes different, so using symbols that are internationally recognised allows chess players of different nationalities to follow the moves printed in books using figurine algebraic notation. The numbering of squares, a1, e4, g7, etc., is the same in most countries.

The following series of diagrams and notes will help you to understand algebraic notation in action.

Set up your board and play them through. Bear in mind that the moves given are not all 'good' moves, but as we are using only King, Bishop and pawn moves we cannot necessarily make what would be better moves at certain points in this example.

This opening sequence is intended only to show you how to read and write down moves in algebraic notation. Black's second and third moves, and White's third and fourth moves are shown in figurine notation with the written algebraic notation following in brackets. All other moves in this sequence are pawn moves; as no symbol is used in pawn moves, the notation shown is as it would appear both in written and figurine algebraic notations.

Check carefully that the pieces on your board are in the same positions as shown in our diagrams. If they are not the same, check back that you have read and made the moves correctly.

 **1 d4  e6**

White takes advantage of being able to move a pawn two squares forward on its first move. Black is satisfied with a single-square move in reply.

 **2 b4**

Another 'two-square' first move for a pawn, but right into the path of Black's King's Bishop standing on f8.

*Diagram 7.1 The position after White's second move.*

 **2 ...  ♗xb4+**

(Bxb4+) Black captures the pawn with his King's Bishop and attacks the white King.

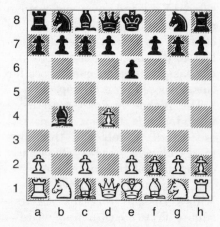

*Diagram 7.2 After Black's second move.*

 **3 ♗d2**

(Bd2) White blocks the check by moving his Queen's Bishop onto a square between his King and the attacking piece. You can see that the King could not move out of check because all the squares around him are occupied by his own pieces.

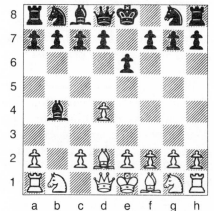

*Diagram 7.3   White has played move 3.*

**3   ...   ♝xd2+**

(Bxd2+) Black captures the defending Bishop and again attacks the King.

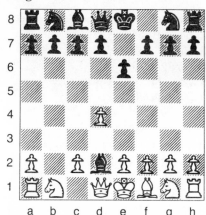

*Diagram 7.4   Both sides have made three moves.*

**4   ♔xd2**

(Kxd2) White's King captures the attacking Bishop.

**4   ...   f5**
**5   e4   f4**

Black does not take the white e-pawn but moves on. He is not attacking the white King, but would be if the King were standing on e3 instead of d2.

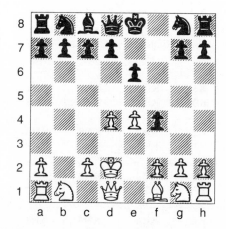

*Diagram 7.5   After five moves by each side.*

**6   g4**

Now Black can, if he wishes, capture this g-pawn en passant – but he must do so immediately.

*Diagram 7.6   Following White's sixth move.*

**6   ...   fxg3 ep**

Yes, Black did want to capture en passant. Note that when we write this move we name the square onto which the black pawn moved and not the square the captured white pawn was occupying.

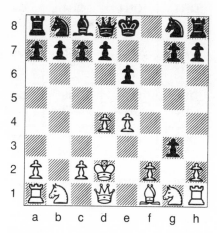

*Diagram 7.7   Both sides have made six moves.*

When you know more about playing chess you will realize how absurd that opening is from a chess point of view. But it did give us a chance to show you the King and the Bishop in symbol form – as they appear in algebraic notation – and how to write down the moves. It also gave you the first opportunity to practise playing through some moves from text diagrams.

In many English-speaking countries, descriptive notation is still popular, and many books exist which are printed in that form. In descriptive notation, each square has two names, one from Black's end of the board and one from White's end. Diagram 7.8 shows each square's two names, Black at the top and White below.

Each file is named after the chess piece that stands on it at the start of a game, and the ranks are numbered according to their distance from each player. Black's QB1 is White's QB8, K5 for Black is K4 for White, and so on. Again, more confusing at first glance than it actually is once you have practised for a while.

To illustrate how moves are shown in the three forms – figurine algebraic, written algebraic and descriptive – here are the six moves used in our opening example (diagrams 7.1 to 7.7) shown in all three ways.

| Queen's Rook's file | Queen's Knight's file | Queen's Bishop's file | Queen's file | King's file | King's Bishop's file | King's Knight's file | King's Rook's file |
|---|---|---|---|---|---|---|---|
| QR1 QR8 | QN1 QN8 | QB1 QB8 | Q1 Q8 | K1 K8 | KB1 KB8 | KN1 KN8 | KR1 KR8 |
| QR2 QR7 | QN2 QN7 | QB2 QB7 | Q2 Q7 | K2 K7 | KB2 KB7 | KN2 KN7 | KR2 KR7 |
| QR3 QR6 | QN3 QN6 | QB3 QB6 | Q3 Q6 | K3 K6 | KB3 KB6 | KN3 KN6 | KR3 KR6 |
| QR4 QR5 | QN4 QN5 | QB4 QB5 | Q4 Q5 | K4 K5 | KB4 kB5 | KN4 KN5 | KR4 KR5 |
| QR5 QR4 | QN5 QN4 | QB5 QB4 | Q5 Q4 | K5 K4 | KB5 KB4 | KN5 KN4 | KR5 KR4 |
| QR6 QR3 | QN6 QN3 | QB6 QB3 | Q6 Q3 | K6 K3 | KB6 KB3 | KN6 KN3 | KR6 KR3 |
| QR7 QR2 | QN7 QN2 | QB7 QB2 | Q7 Q2 | K7 K2 | KB7 KB2 | KN7 KN2 | KR7 KR2 |
| QR8 QR1 | QN8 QN1 | QB8 QB1 | Q8 Q1 | K8 K1 | KB8 KB1 | KN8 KN1 | KR8 KR1 |

1 d4    e6
2 b4    ♝xb4+
3 ♝d2   ♝xd2+
4 ♚xd2  f5
5 e4    f4
6 g4    fxg3 ep

1 d4    e6
2 b4    Bxb4+
3 Bd2   Bxd2+
4 Kxd2  f5
5 e4    f4
6 g4    fxg3 ep

1 P-Q4   P-K3
2 P-QN4  BxP+ (or) BxP ch
3 B-Q2   BxB+ (or) BxB ch
4 KxB    P-KB4
5 P-K4   P-B5
6 P-N4   PxP ep

*Diagram 7.8  Showing the two names given to each square in descriptive notation*

From that little exercise you will

probably have spotted the main differences between algebraic and descriptive notation. In descriptive, the pawn *is* identified by a capital P; there is a short line (-) showing 'moves to'; as well as a plus sign (+) check can be shown as 'ch'; it is necessary to show if certain moves are made on the King's side or the Queen's side of the board to avoid confusion. For example, Black's move 4 . . . P-KB4. We had to show it was a King's Bishop's pawn move as both Bishop's pawns could have moved to their respective B4 squares. But on move 5 . . . P-B5, this clarification was unnecessary as the Queen's Bishop's pawn could not reach its B5 square on that move.

The only other main difference is that sometimes, in descriptive notation, the Knight is abbreviated to Kt instead of N.

We strongly recommend you learn both forms of notation as books using either style are available, and it would be foolish to deny yourself access to the games and instruction in some of them for the sake of a little commonsense practice now.

## Questions on Unit 7

Give the answers in (a) algebraic (b) descriptive notation.

1   What symbol is used to denote 'check'?

2   How would you write down 'a white pawn on e4 captures a black pawn on d5'?

3   The black King moves one square forward from the square upon which he started the game. Write down this move.

4   There is a white pawn on b5 and Black moves his pawn from a7 to a5. White captures this pawn with his b-pawn. Write down White's move.

5   With a pawn on f7, White captures a Rook on g8 and promotes to a Knight, which immediately places the black King in check. Write down this move.

\*          \*          \*

One of the greatest chess players the world has known was Emanuel Lasker (1868–1941). Lasker once said 'Properly taught, a student of chess can learn more in a few hours than he would find out in ten years of untutored trial and error'.

Although he was acknowledged as chess champion of the world from 1894 to 1921, Lasker was primarily a mathematician, and in his later years devoted himself to philosophy, but he often felt the urge to play competitive chess. He played in his last international tournament in 1936, at the age of 68.

\*          \*          \*

## Answers to questions on Unit 7

|   | (a) | (b) |
|---|-----|-----|
| 1 | + | + or ch |
| 2 | exd5 | PxP |
| 3 | . . . Ke7 | . . . K-K2 |
| 4 | bxa6 ep | PxP ep |
| 5 | fxg8=N+ | PxR=N+ |
|   |  | or PxR=N ch |

# Unit 8

## King and Pawn Exercises

Although there are sometimes several pieces left in the end game it often comes down to just Kings and pawns. Since a pawn can promote to a piece with which you can probably give checkmate it is obviously very important to learn how to make the best use of your King and pawns. A lone pawn, even with the King's help, cannot checkmate.

Suppose you have a pawn left, while your opponent has only his King. The lone King will naturally try to stop your pawn from promoting, so your King must shepherd the pawn through to the promotion square. Your King must therefore gain control of the promotion square, while at the same time guarding the pawn from the enemy King.

This Unit contains exercises that will teach you about this most important part of end-game play. Study these exercises carefully and practise them until you have an idea of which types of end-game positions are better for you.

Once you realize which types of end-game positions you can win

from it will be easier for you to make decisions in the middle game that will give you a better chance of reaching the end game with an advantage.

Your opponent will of course be trying to get the advantage for himself, so generally victory will go to the player with the better understanding of how to play the end game. This is why we are placing so much importance on your gaining experience and knowledge of how best to use your King and pawns in an end game, even before we deal with how the other pieces move.

In the first exercise we have given you the solutions, together with some comments, so that you can see exactly how you are expected to use this practice.

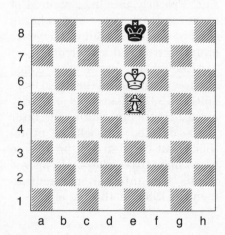

*Diagram 8.1  With Black to play, does the pawn promote?*

## Solution

1 ... Kd8
2 Kf7 Kd7
3 e6+ Kd8
4 e7+ Kd7
5 e8=Q+

and White has promoted to a Queen. **or**

1 ... Kf8
2 Kd7 Kf7
3 e6+ Kf8
4 e7+ Kf7
5 e8=Q+

and White does it again. Notice that in both cases White moved his King in the opposite direction from Black, so that he could gain control of the promotion square without interference from the black King.

Now try with White to play first.

## Solution

1 Kd6 Kd8
2 e6 Ke8
3 e7 Kf7
4 Kd7

and White does it yet again.

Black loses control of the 'Queening' square and whatever he plays White will promote next move.

Set up the position again and try making different moves with either or both colours. Unless the player with the white pieces 'commits suicide' there is no way that Black can stop him promoting his pawn. Try 1 Kf6 for White, or 1 Kd5, or 1 Kf5.

Try everything – you can't get too much practice.

Although we show White as the attacker and Black with the lone King in these exercises, do not get the idea that the White pieces are in any way superior or special. If you reverse the positions to the opposite end of the board – giving Black the pawn instead of White – the principles of how to play these endings would remain exactly the same.

In these exercises we are not concerned with going on to checkmate the lone King after promoting the pawn. You will need to know how the pieces move before we can show you that far. Our concern in this unit is simply showing you how to get a pawn through to promotion.

Often a player facing a King and Queen with a lone King will resign (give up the game), since he would realize that he can't avoid being checkmated. In fact you will encounter even earlier resignations – when a player sees that he can't stop his opponent promoting a pawn. We advise you *not* to resign in such a position, at least while you are still learning. It is easy to make a mistake, so play all your exercises and games through to the very end. Both you and your opponent will benefit from the practice of actually making the moves and anticipating the replies. You will almost certainly make some mistakes as well, so don't be too self-confident – even when you think you have an easily won game.

Many games that a player seemed to be winning easily have been thrown away because of a careless move (remember stalemate, for example?). It is easy to relax your concentration when you think you are winning, so be sure *you* don't fall into this trap. You may sometimes be able to find other ways of tackling the positions than the ways we suggest, but remember that in chess you should always look for the shortest, safest route to victory, and not a long way round, even though the longer route may be 'prettier' or more flashy.

Now set up the pieces diagram by diagram for the rest of the exercises in this Unit. Be careful to ensure that you place the correct pieces on the actual squares named. (You may have noticed, while playing through some earlier diagrams, how easy it is to make a mistake when setting up or moving pieces.)

## Exercises

(Solutions at end of Unit)

Diagram 8.2 (a) White to play. (b) Black to play. Does the pawn promote whoever has the first move?
Diagram 8.3 (a) White to play. (b) Black to play. Does the pawn promote in either case?
Diagram 8.4 (a) White to play. (b) Black to play. What is the result in each case?

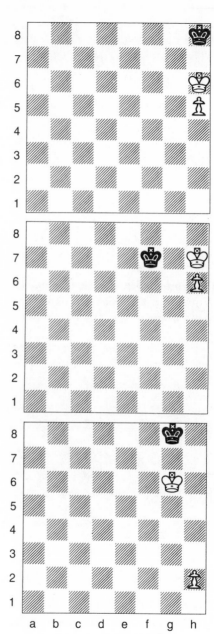

*Diagrams 8.2, 8.3 and 8.4*

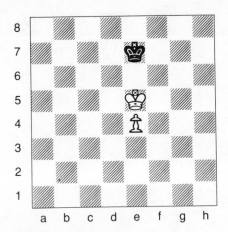

*Diagram 8.5*

Diagram 8.5 (a) Black to play. (b) White to play. Does the pawn promote whoever has the first move?

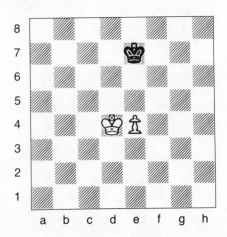

*Diagram 8.6*

Diagram 8.6 (a) White to play. (b) Black to play. What are the results?

\*　　　\*　　　\*

You may have wondered why the Knight in a chess set and in diagrams takes the shape of a horse's head.

This is because in the original game of 'chaturanga' this piece was, in fact, a horse ('ashwa'). As the game moved on, and other pieces were changed, the horse remained. In Persia it was called an 'asp' and the Arabs called it 'faras', both meaning a horse. When the game reached Europe, in early medieval times, this piece came under the influence of the founding of chivalric orders and became known in most European countries as a Knight. However, in Spain ('caballo') and Russia ('kon') it is still a horse, and the Germans call it a 'Springer'.

As you learn how this piece moves you will see just how appropriate the German name is, for this is the *only* piece that can jump over other pieces on the chessboard. You will also realize that, for this reason, the Knight is the only piece — apart of course from the pawn – that could possibly make the first move in a chess game.

\*　　　\*　　　\*

## Solutions

Diagram 8.2 (a)

| | | |
|---|---|---|
| 1 | Kg6 | Kg8 |
| 2 | h6 | Kh8 |
| 3 | h7 | |

stalemate, so the pawn cannot promote.

Diagram 8.2 (b)

| | | |
|---|---|---|
| 1 | ... | Kg8 |
| 2 | Kg6 | Kh8 |
| 3 | h6 | Kg8 |
| 4 | h7+ | Kh8 |

stalemate and again no pawn promotion. Whoever has first move, Black can always reach a stalemate because as play is on a Rook file (an outside file) Black's 'escape' moves are limited. In this case these limitations work in Black's favour, since if he were able to 'escape' White would promote and eventually effect checkmate. Take special care with endings involving play on the Rook files.

Diagram 8.3 (a)

| | | |
|---|---|---|
| 1 | Kh8 | Kf8 |
| 2 | h7 | Kf7 |

stalemate. This time it is the white King who has no legal move, but the result is still, despite his pawn advantage, a draw.

Diagram 8.3 (b)

| | | |
|---|---|---|
| 1 | ... | Kf8 |
| 2 | Kh8 | Kf7 |
| 3 | h7 | Kf8 |

stalemate again. You can try out any other series of moves that may be possible and will find that Black can *always* reach stalemate from this type of starting position, either by keeping White's King in front of the pawn or by putting his own King there.

Diagram 8.4 (a)

| | | |
|---|---|---|
| 1 | h4 | Kh8 |
| 2 | h5 | Kg8 |
| 3 | h6 | Kh8 |
| 4 | h7 | |

stalemate. By now you should recognize this final position – after all, we have encountered it in playing through the previous two diagrams.

The same thing will happen with Black to play first, diag. 8.4 (b), because Black can always keep popping into the corner and White's King can never gain control of this square to promote his pawn.

Diagram 8.5 (a)

| | | |
|---|---|---|
| 1 | ... | Kd7 |
| 2 | Kf6 | Ke8 |
| 3 | Ke6 | Kd8 |
| 4 | Kf7 | |

and White wins because wherever Black now moves his King, the white pawn cannot be stopped from reaching e8, since his own King is controlling that square. (You know that the Kings can never occupy adjoining squares.) We know from diag. 8.1, for instance, that once the white King occupies e6 and the pawn is behind him, White wins whoever has the move. It is not always so easy, however. . . .

Diagram 8.5 (b)  The same starting position as diag. 8.5 (a), of course, but this time with White to play first.

| | | |
|---|---|---|
| 1 | Kd5 | Kd7 |
| 2 | e5 | Ke7 |
| 3 | e6 | Ke8 |
| 4 | Kd6 | Kd8 |
| 5 | e7+ | Ke8 |
| 6 | Ke6 | |

stalemate. This may seem surprising, so why don't you try other series of moves for yourself? See if you can promote the white pawn when White has first move.

Play this against another player, changing ends so that you both get a chance to try to promote the pawn or defend the position. Compare this situation with diag. 8.1. You should, as White, try every possible move to force the pawn through, and as Black, set every possible trap until you can play this position blind-fold. Can you think of a rule for defending this type of position?

Diagram 8.6 (a)

**1  Ke5**

and we have the position in diag. 8.5, which you know that White can win, since it will now be Black's move. You should make sure that no other move than 1 Ke5 will result in a win from the position shown in diag. 8.6 (it won't). If you have done your work properly on diag. 8.5, you will have no problem in defending this position against any other move.

Diagram 8.6 (b)

| | | |
|---|---|---|
| | 1 | ... | Kd6 |
| or | 1 | ... | Ke6 |

Both draw because they prevent the advance of White's King. A bad move would be 1 ... Kd7?, since after 2 Kd5 Ke7 3 Ke5! White has reached the winning position in diag. 8.5 (a).

You need practice, practice, and more practice. When you think you fully understand the principles shown in these examples, try inventing some positions to start from and see whether or not you can promote the pawn. You will certainly have promoted yourself – to a much better end-game player – and will be better than many who have not paid so much attention to the things you have learned in these examples.

Just stop for a minute and think how much you *have* learned and how much fun you have had, simply by using Kings and pawns. Can you imagine what treats lie in store for you now as you learn how to use the more powerful pieces?

# Unit 9

## The Knight

Knights and Bishops are known as 'minor' pieces because they are (usually) less powerful than either the Rook or the Queen.

Most beginners love the Knight, and his move (he is the only piece that can jump over other pieces) is quite delightful. Sometimes it seems that he is waltzing to a romantic melody while on other occasions he gives the impression that he is charging through a crowded battlefield with his rider cutting down the enemies that stand in his way.

The Knight's move may at first seem tricky, but it is really very simple. He moves two squares up or down a file and then – in the same move – one square to either side. Alternatively he moves two squares along a rank and then one square up or down.

Two ways to help you remember this move are (i) that it is an L-shaped move, and (ii) that the Knight lands on a square of the *opposite* colour to the one from which he started his leap.

The best way to get the Knight's

move fixed firmly in your mind is to practise it on your own board – after a while you will have no trouble at all in remembering it.

In diag. 9.1 White's King's Knight is shown on the square he occupies at the start of a game – g1 – a *black* square, from where he can control three *white* squares.

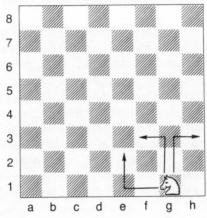

Diagram 9.1

Let us say that his first move took him from g1 to h3. How many squares can he control from here? Use your own board and a Knight to find this out. Remember that he is now standing on h3, a white square, so the squares he controls must be black.

One of them is the square he has just left – g1. Another L-shaped move can take him from h3 to f2, and you will quickly see that from h3 he can also reach f4 and g5. So from h3 he can control a total of four squares.

What if he had moved from g1 to e2. How many squares could he control from here?

e2 is a white square, so we know that the squares he would be controlling must be black, as was the case from h3, and again one of them is the square he has just left – g1. The total number of squares he could control from e2 is six – c1, c3, d4, f4, g3 and g1.

Now let us see how many squares this Knight would control had he occupied f3. Place your Knight on this square and see if you can list the squares – there are no less than *eight* this time.

Have you found them? e1, d2, d4, e5, g5, h4, h2 and g1.

It should be obvious that the Knight can control more squares from any of the sixteen squares in the centre of the board than he can from any other square. From any of the central sixteen squares he can control a maximum of eight other squares, while he is reduced to controlling 6, 4, 3 or even only 2 (try him from any of the four corner squares) when he is on the two outside rows.

Diagram 9.2 shows this clearly. The numbers printed in the two outside ranks and files indicate how many squares the Knight can control from each of these squares. The blank sixteen squares in the centre of the board are those from which he can control his maximum number of eight.

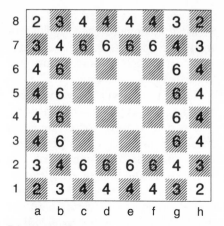

Diagram 9.2

As you learn more about opening chess games you will find that White often develops his King's Knight to f3 and his Queen's Knight to c3 for maximum control, and that Black often places his Knights on f6 and c6 for the same reason.

The following exercise shows how

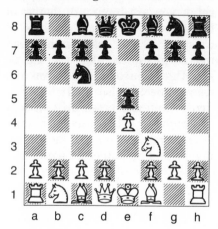

Diagram 9.3

Knights are often developed in the opening.

Set up your pieces to start a game. Now play –

> 1 e4 e5
> 2 Nf3 Nc6

You will notice that when White played Nf3 he not only developed the Knight towards the centre of the board, he also attacked Black's pawn on e5. With 2 . . . Nc6, Black also developed his Knight towards the centre, and at the same time protected his e-pawn.

Now is a good time to point out to you that everything in chess is 'relative'. This means that what may be thought of as the 'best' square for a certain piece to occupy depends upon the state of the game, or upon a particular position.

Let us say, for example, that from the position shown in diag. 9.4 it is Black to play.

He will obviously move his pawn

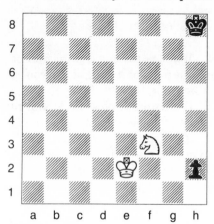

Diagram 9.4

to h1 and promote it to a Queen. In this case, White's Knight on f3 – though controlling his maximum of eight squares – is useless. But if he were on f2 or g3, he would be controlling the 'Queening' square and Black would not be able to promote.

Because of his ability to jump over other pieces, the Knight is obviously very useful on a crowded board. Even if he is surrounded by pieces of both sides he can still leap them and either go to the aid of his own pieces or threaten the enemy.

Look carefully at diag. 9.5 and before you read on take a piece of paper and write down which of the eight squares that the Knight *could* reach are actually available to him.

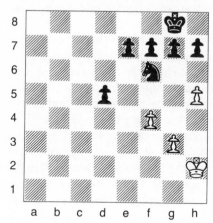

Diagram 9.5

Well, we know that the eight squares e4, d5, d7, e8, g8, h7, h5 and g4 are all within reach of the Knight on f6. Three of these squares are not available to him in the position shown in diag. 9.5, since they are occupied by his own pieces – a pawn on d5, the King on g8 and a pawn on h7. This leaves five squares open to him – e4, d7, e8 and g4, which are unoccupied, and h5 because he could capture the white pawn on this square. Did you name all five squares?

Did you notice anything important about the effect of moving the Knight from f6 to g4? What squares would he be attacking from g4? Well, one of them is h2 – and the enemy King is standing on that square. So if the Knight moved from f6 to g4 he would then be attacking the King, i.e. the King would be in check, and White would have to do something about it on his very next move.

In Unit 6 we mentioned that there were three ways to get a King out of check. In this particular case the only one open to the white King is to move to a square that is not attacked by an enemy piece.

The black Knight on g4 could not be captured and – a *very* important point to remember – when a Knight places the King in check *nothing* can interpose (block the check) because of the Knight's jumping move.

Set up the position shown in diag. 9.6 on your board.

Let us say that you have just moved a pawn from f7 to f8 and have chosen to promote to a Knight, so that you can immediately give

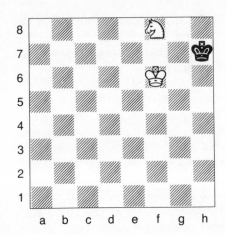

*Diagram 9.6*

check to the black King. Now all you have to do is make it *checkmate*. Try. What happens? What have you learned about the Knight in this situation?

Give yourself about five minutes. If you have not succeeded in checkmating the black King by then, look at the solution.

## Questions on Unit 9

1   What is the maximum number of squares that a Knight can control at any one time?
2   If a Knight gives check, can the check be blocked by interposing?
3   If a Knight moves from a white square, what will be the colour of the square he lands on?
4   Is the Knight considered to be a major or a minor piece?

\*       \*       \*

Once you have learned how to play chess, and how to read and write down the moves, there are many ways in which you can put this knowledge to good use.

Not only can you play over-the-board games against an opponent, you can also play correspondence chess, set or solve chess problems, play through the games of the 'great' (and the 'not so great') players of the past and present, or you may even choose to write about the game. You may want to do all of these things.

Whichever way you decide to use your knowledge of chess, you will always be glad that you learned to play the game soundly from the very beginning. This is what we hope to achieve with the Pitman Chess Teaching Scheme.

Whatever you do, *don't* get disheartened when you lose a game, when you make a mistake, or if you think you are having difficulty in understanding certain aspects of chess. Everyone loses games and makes mistakes, and you can be sure that some of the ideas you find easy someone else is finding difficult – and vice versa. Just stick at it. Study, practise and play, and sooner or later you will be a chess player and no longer a beginner.

\*       \*       \*

## Answers to Questions on Unit 9

| | | | |
|---|---|---|---|
| 1 | Eight. | 3 | Black. |
| 2 | No. | 4 | A minor piece. |

*Solution to diag. 9.6*

You will have found that to give checkmate with only a King and a Knight is just not possible. Obviously you would not have promoted your successful pawn to a Knight had you known this before, but do not think that we were treating you unfairly by asking you to try to checkmate. The best way to learn anything is to try it for yourself, and that is exactly what you did in this case. We hope you will continue to do so right through the book!

# Unit 10

## The Bishop

This other minor piece has a very different move from the Knight. While the Knight jumps to a square of the opposite colour, the Bishop *always* stays on squares of the same colour. To do this he must move *diagonally*.

The Bishop can, in a single move, pass over any number of unoccupied squares in a straight line. He cannot jump over pieces – either of his own side or his enemy's

He can capture an enemy piece that stands in his way – if he wishes to – but he must then, of course, take its place. He cannot continue past that square in the same move.

## Exercises

1 Place a white Bishop on f8. From here how many moves would this Bishop need to get to each of the following squares from f8? a1, a7, b4, d8, g7, h6, h7, and h8.

In Unit 9 (diag. 9.6) having promoted a pawn to a Knight on f8, you tried to checkmate a lone enemy King, only to find it impossible to achieve.

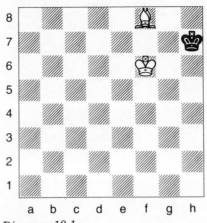

Diagram 10.1

In diagram 10.1, we have the same position except that the pawn has been promoted to a Bishop. Can you give checkmate now? Try a few moves before reading on.

You probably realised very quickly that since each Bishop only controls squares of one colour, even with his King in close attendance he could not cover all the escape squares.

But what if the possible escape squares were occupied? Look at diagram 10.2.

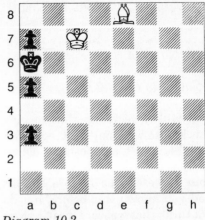

Diagram 10.2

The white Bishop can give checkmate in three moves. Write down this sequence of moves.

If you play the first move for White correctly, you will then be able to force all Black's subsequent moves.

## Solutions

*1* In *one* move the Bishop could reach the squares g7, h6 or b4. In *two* moves he could reach h8, a1, a7 or d8. He could never reach h7, of course, since this is a different colour from f8.

*Diagram 10.2* This exercise tests not only your ability to use a Bishop well but also your ability to sum up a situation properly.

The first thing you should have noted was that the black King was on a white square – the same colour as the attacking Bishop. Black would, therefore, avoid any chance of being checkmated if he could move his King to a black square. In fact, unless White did something about it, Black would move his pawn from a5 to a4, leaving a5 – which is a *black* square – free for his King to escape to.

So White stops that tactic by playing 1 Ba4, blocking the way for the pawn on a5. Black is then forced to play 1 ... a2 (his King is still unable to move). White aims to keep it that way, and plays 2 Kc6. It does not matter that the only move left open to Black is 2 ... a1=Q. White does not care about Black promoting, because all he has to do now is to play 3 Bb5 and Black is checkmated.

That exercise should indicate that there are many different possibilities in a game of chess. It is up to you to recognize the best one in each situation and exploit it to the full.

## Questions on Unit 10

1 Upon what colour square does White's King's Bishop start a game?
2 Could Black's Queen's Bishop ever make a capture on a3?
3 How many different squares could a Bishop reach in one move from e4? (provided of course that the squares concerned were unoccupied).
4 How many squares could a Bishop reach from a1?

5 What would happen if, from the position shown in diag. 10.1, play continued 1 ... Kh8 2 Bg7+ Kh7 3 Kf7?

\*     \*     \*

When you enter certain chess tournaments you will be expected to use a chess clock.

Some players are nervous when using such a clock for the first time – so much so that it can even put them off their game. They are nervous only because the idea of a chess clock and the reasons for its use have never been fully explained to them, but once you understand these things you need not be concerned about using a clock yourself.

Until some form of timing device was introduced to the game, players could take a long time over their moves, and consequently some games went on for days! There were also cases where one of the players would take much more time than his opponent, which was of course most unfair.

The first timing devices used were hour-glasses filled with sand; mechanical clocks were introduced during the nineteenth century. Towards the end of the century the first mechanical 'double' chess clock was invented, and variations of this have been used ever since. The photograph shows a typical chess clock of the type used today in clubs, schools and at tournaments.

*This photograph shows a chess clock set (at 5.30) for the start of a game. Note that the buttons on the top of the clock are level – therefore neither clock is going.*

*White has lost on time. You can see that his 'flag' has fallen because the minute hand has reached the '12' and his 30 minutes have all been used up.*

*Black still has a few minutes left, but you can see that the minute hand has started to lift his 'flag'.*

*Note that Black's button is depressed and White's is up, showing that White's clock is in motion.*

Let us say that a total of one hour is allowed for a particular game. Each player has 30 minutes of that hour in which to make the required number of moves, according to the rules of the match or tournament, unless of course the game is won or a draw is agreed before either player has reached the time limit.

You will see there is a small plastic strip near the top of each clock face. This is called the 'flag', and as the minute hand approaches the top of the face (where the figure 12 would be on a normal clock, and *is* on some chess clocks) it lifts the flag. When the minute hand reaches the 12, the flag drops, and the player concerned has used up all his time. If he has not played the required number of moves – or more – he loses on time. The other small plastic strip on each clock face moves back and forth when that clock is in motion.

You will also see two buttons on the top of the clock, one at each end. When these are level neither clock is going, and this is of course how you find them at the start of a game.

Before a game commences, a tournament controller sets each clock at a time suitable to the time limit for that particular game. If we still think of each player as having 30 minutes, the clock might be set to show 5.30 (regardless of the actual time of day), so that the flag can come into operation after 30 minutes.

When the players are told to start their clocks, the player with the Black pieces presses his button, which immediately starts his opponent's clock. Once White has made his move, he presses the button on his side of the clock, stopping his clock and starting his opponent's. Black, once his move is made, repeats the process, and so on, each player stopping his own clock and automatically starting his opponent's after each move that he makes.

This means that each player can think about his opponent's *last* move only on his *own* time, although he can (and does) naturally think about the general situation while his opponent's clock is going.

It is advisable to own a chess clock yourself and to use it whenever you play a game against anyone – even a friendly game. This way you will quickly get used to using the clock and it should cause you no problem when you play in a tournament, etc. It also avoids any disagreement between yourself and your opponent as to who took the longer time to think about and make his moves. It is fair to both sides.

Chess clocks like the one shown in the photograph have been in use for many years and will continue to be in use for a long time to come. Recently, however, there has been a natural progression towards electronic digital clocks, but it will probably be some years before they are sufficiently inexpensive to be brought into general use.

\*  \*  \*

## Answers to Questions on Unit 10

1    White.
2    No. Black's Queen's Bishop operates on white squares and the square a3 is black.
3    13 – d5, c6, b7 and a8; f5, g6 and h7; f3, g2 and h1; d3, c2 and b1.
4    7 – b2, c3, d4, e5, f6, g7 and h8.
5    Stalemate.

# Unit 11

## The Rook

Like the Bishop, this major piece also moves in straight lines. But while the Bishop moves diagonally, the Rook moves up and down the files or across the ranks.

The Rook captures like any other piece – by removing the captured piece from the board and taking over the square upon which it had been standing.

He cannot jump over pieces, so – like the Bishop – his moves are restricted to the number of squares open to him before he comes to an occupied square.

Diagrams 11.1 to 11.5 give examples of how the Rook can and cannot move. When you have studied them, play through the exercises and you will begin to understand just how useful this powerful major piece can be.

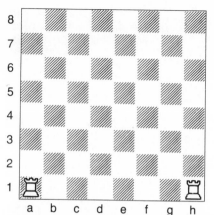

*Diagram 11.1   White's Rook on a1 could, in a single move, go to any square along the rank – except h1, which is already occupied by White's other Rook. The Rook on h1 could similarly move to any square along the rank – except a1. Both Rooks could move anywhere along the file upon which they stand — from a2 to a8 in the case of the Queen's Rook, from h2 to h8 in the case of the King's Rook.*

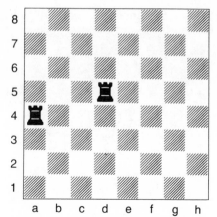

*Diagram 11.2   In this diagram Black's Rooks are nearer to the centre of the board, but their moving powers remain*

the same. The Rook on a4 commands the a-file and the 4th rank, while his colleague on d5 looks after the d-file and the 5th rank.

If all the squares on the rank and file upon which a Rook was standing were empty, the Rook would always control 14 squares from anywhere on the board. This is one reason why the Rook is called a major piece. Bishops and Knights are less powerful from the corner or the edge of the board.

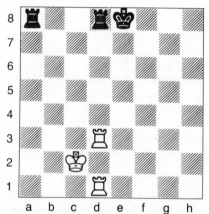

*Diagram 11.3   Here if it were White to move, he could take Black's Rook on d8 and give check to the King – 1 Rxd8+. The black King could not recapture, since the white Rook on d1 would be protecting the other white Rook on d8, and, as you know, the King cannot move into check. But Black's Rook on a8 could recapture, 1 ... Rxd8 – and would be protected by the King, for if White were to play 2 Rxd8, Black would simply reply 2 ... Kxd8 and both sides would have given up two Rooks. A fair exchange perhaps, but in this particular situation only the Kings would be left and the game would therefore be drawn.*

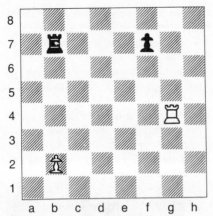

Diagram 11.4 Here White's Rook controls his full quota of 14 squares, while Black's Rook controls only 10. Black cannot get past e7 along the rank, since his own pawn on f7 stops him. He can, however, capture the white pawn on b2.

While the white Rook on g4 could move to any one of 14 squares, he would not be advised to move to g6, since the pawn on f7 could then capture him. Similarly neither Rook would be advised to move to b4, since the other Rook could then make a capture. In each instance a piece would be lost for nothing.

## Exercises

1  Place a Rook on f8. With the rest of the board clear, what is the *maximum* number of moves this Rook would need to reach any particular square?

Diagram 11.5 You have already learned about promoting a successful pawn to a Knight or a Bishop.

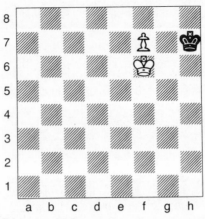

Diagram 11.5

Now you decide to promote to a Rook. So 1 f8=R. Could you checkmate this time? If so, how many moves would you need?

Diagram 11.6 White to play. How many moves must White make before he has checkmated the black King?

Does the enemy King have to be

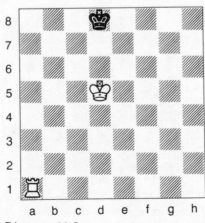

Diagram 11.6

at the edge of the board to be checkmated by a King and a Rook?

(If you cannot checkmate fairly quickly, look at the answer to this exercise before you try the following exercises. There are tricks in every trade.)

Diagram 11.7 White to move and checkmate. There is more than one way to do this, but provided you effect checkmate it doesn't really matter how you do it in this particular case.

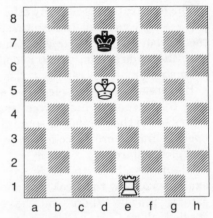

Diagram 11.7

It is always best to finish off a game as quickly as possible because as long as you are playing there is a chance that you will make a mistake.

The quickest way to mate from diag. 11.7 is in seven moves, but in the solution we also show you a ten-move mate, so see what you can do.

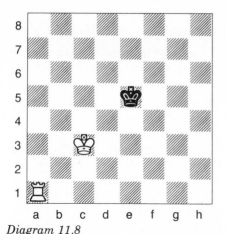

*Diagram 11.8*

*Diagram 11.8* With White to play, see if you can checkmate the black King in less than 15 moves. Write down the moves made for both sides.

*Exercise 2* Now go back to diag. 11.3, where White exchanged both Rooks and got a draw. Can you find something better for him from this position?

## Solutions

Exercise 1 The Rook on f8 could reach any square on a clear board in a maximum of two moves. The Bishop, you will remember, can reach any square of *his own colour* in two moves, but the Rook can reach any square of *either* colour. This doesn't make the Rook twice as powerful as the Bishop, but make no mistake about it he *is* a very powerful piece indeed.

Diagram 11.5 You could mate in one move, once you had promoted to a Rook. The Knight couldn't do it, the Bishop couldn't do it, but the Rook could. From the diagram position, 1 f8=R Kh6 (forced, there is nowhere else the King could go) 2 Rh8 mate.

But what if the black King had been on h8 when White promoted? This would have meant 1 f8=R+, forcing Black to play 1 ... Kh7. Now White could not mate straight away, but as long as the Rook stayed on the 8th rank Black's King would have to go to h6 next move anyway.

So the white Rook needs a 'waiting' move and this could be obtained by his moving to a8, b8, c8, d8 or e8. Any of these moves would stop the black King from going back to h8, and since White's King is controlling g5, g6 and g7, Black could only move to h6, whereupon the Rook would move to h8 and mate as before.

You will often find in Rook endings the need for a waiting move. Make sure that you understand exactly what a waiting move means in these circumstances, since it will win many a game for you in the future. Like most things it is really quite easy when you know how!

Diagram 11.6 White could mate in three moves. 1 Kd6, and Black has a choice of two replies. If 1 ... Kc8 2 Rb1 Kd8 3 Rb8 mate. If 1 ...

Ke8 2 Rf1 Kd8 3 Rf8 mate. The Rook's move to cover the b-file in the first variation and the f-file in the second stopped the black King from escaping and drove him back to d8 in each case, so that he could be mated next move, the white King already blocking the possible escape squares on the 7th rank.

The answer to the second part of the question is *yes*. There is no way of mating with only a King and a Rook unless the enemy king is at the edge of the board.

Diagram 11.7 The quickest way to mate would go something like this –

| 1 | Kc5 | Kc7 |
|---|-----|-----|
| 2 | Re7+ | Kd8 |
| 3 | Kd6 | Kc8 |
| 4 | Rh7 | Kb8 |

(... Kd8 would allow mate next move, of course)

| 5 | Kc6 | Ka8 |
|---|-----|-----|
| 6 | Kb6 | Kb8 |
| 7 | Rh8 | |

mate. (White's 4th move – Rh7 – stopped the black King from escaping through the b7 square.)

An alternative way to mate could be the following –

| 1 | Re2 | Kc7 |
|---|-----|-----|
| 2 | Re7+ | Kb6 |
| 3 | Rf7 ('waiting') | Kb5 |
| 4 | Rb7+ | Ka6 |
| 5 | Rb1 | Ka5 |
| 6 | Kc4 | Ka6 |
| 7 | Kc5 | Ka7 |
| 8 | Kc6 | Ka8 |
| 9 | Kc7 | Ka7 |

**10  Ra1**

mate.

The second way is a little longer than the first, but it has its own method and the result is the same. The black King is forced to the edge of the board (which edge doesn't matter – it can be left to the black King himself to choose his own resting place; all we are doing is forcing him to rest somewhere), and mate is effected by the Rook when the Kings are facing one another.

The most likely mistake for a beginner to make is for him to forget that useful waiting move.

Diagram 11.8  Whenever you are shown a series of moves as the solution to a chess problem, you may well wonder what would have happened if one or both of the players had made different moves to the ones shown. It is obviously impractical to give all the possible variations move after move, and such analysis as is given is usually either the best series of moves by both players under the circumstances or just an example of how play might continue from a given position. The suggested series of moves in this exercise is –

| | | |
|---|---|---|
| 1 | Re1+ | Kf5 |
| 2 | Kd4 | Kf4 |
| 3 | Re4+ | Kf5 |
| | (Rf1+ is also good) | |
| 4 | Kd5 | Kf6 |
| 5 | Re5 | Kf7 |
| | (Rf4+ is also good) | |

| | | |
|---|---|---|
| 6 | Re6 | Kg7 |
| | (Rf5+ or Kd6 are also sensible moves) | |
| 7 | Ke5 | Kf7 |
| 8 | Kf5 | Kg7 |
| 9 | Re7+ | Kf8 |
| 10 | Kf6 | Kg8 |
| 11 | Rb7 (waiting) | Kh8 |
| 12 | Kg6 | Kg8 |
| 13 | Rb8 | |

mate. This shows that it *is* possible to effect checkmate in less than 15 moves – certainly in less than twenty – even when starting from a position in which the enemy King is located firmly in the centre of the board.

It is always important to use the Rook to his full capacity – sometimes to make a waiting move (like 11 Rb7), sometimes to effect a check, forcing the enemy King off a certain rank or file, and sometimes to move the King when the Rook needs some support (since he cannot cover *all* the escape squares or effect checkmate alone).

*Exercise 2*  There is definitely something better for White in diag. 11.3. He can effect checkmate with his two Rooks. One Rook gives check (on e3 or e1), followed by the other Rook until Black is mated, e.g.

| | | |
|---|---|---|
| 1 | Re3+ | Kf7 |
| 2 | Rf1+ | Kg6 |
| 3 | Rg3+ | Kh5 |
| 4 | Rh1 | mate. |

\*      \*      \*

As we have referred to the pieces as 'chessmen' you may have wondered what a Queen is doing with so much fighting power in what is usually regarded as a man's world – the battlefield.

Certainly, apart from obvious exceptions such as Boadicea and Joan of Arc, history mentions few women who have actually led armies into battle.

The explanation is that in the original game 'chaturanga' this piece was merely a Minister or adviser to the King and in fact had very limited powers, being able to move only one square diagonally. Later the move was increased to three squares, but it was not until medieval times that the piece became known as the Queen.

No doubt having regard to the powers of the Queen in a medieval court, where she occupied the throne next to the King and had a great deal of influence in many matters, her powers were increased to those she enjoys today.

\*      \*      \*

# Unit 12

## The Queen

She is your most powerful piece – powerful because she can move like both the Rook *and* the Bishop.

The Queen can move forwards, backwards, sideways and diagonally, so she can threaten a lot of things at the same time. However – like the Rook and the Bishop – she cannot jump over pieces. This particular feat belongs only to the Knight.

Because she is so powerful, you must look after your Queen carefully and always have great respect for your opponent's Queen.

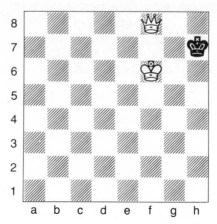

Diagram 12.1

*Diagram 12.1* Standing on d4 the Queen controls no less than 27 squares! Check them for yourself – whole length of
the diagonal    a1 to h8=7 squares
whole length of
the diagonal    g1 to a7=6 squares
the d-file                =7 squares
the 4th rank             =7 squares
                a total of 27 squares

The Queen controls this amount of territory from any of the four centre squares. Even from a corner square she can control 21 squares.

Like the Rook, the Queen can reach any square on the board in one, or at most two moves.

So much power, as well as being useful, can also bring its problems.

*Diagram 12.2* shows the promotion of a pawn to a Queen on f8. What does Black play?

In fact he can't play anything at all! It is stalemate, so in this particular case the tremendous power of the Queen has worked against her. Why is this? If we refer to diag. 11.5, we can see that when the f-pawn was promoted to a Rook, the black King could move to h6. But since the Queen can move like the Bishop as well as the Rook, the black King is denied even this escape square.

This then is one of the times when you would *not* 'Queen' your pawn – you would promote to a Rook instead.

Mating a lone King with a King and Queen is very simple – so simple, in fact, that when faced with such odds many players resign. But some players do *not* resign, so you must make sure that you know how to achieve this simple mate accurately and in the least number of moves (in case you have to do it when you have only a limited time left in a particular game).

Stalemate is obviously a danger. With your Queen able to control so many squares you can easily stalemate your opponent, and you can imagine how annoying that can be when you are a whole Queen up!

The best way to mate a lone King with a King and Queen is to cut down the enemy King's escape squares – restrict the number of moves he can make – without stalemating him, in as few moves as possible.

Diagram 12.2

*Diagram 12.3* gives us a chance to show how to effect checkmate when the enemy King is in the middle of the board.

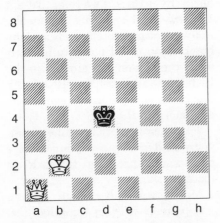

*Diagram 12.3*

We obviously have to drive the King to the edge of the board, because, even with her tremendous powers, the Queen alone cannot effect checkmate. When we get the enemy King to the edge we will still need help from our own King to administer the final blow. With White to play see if you can checkmate in less than ten moves. (Solution at end of Unit.)

*Diagram 12.4* Whatever White plays first, Black will have a number of replies to choose from. Play out as many King and Queen versus King endings as you want to – against another player – so that you get the idea of accurately cutting down the enemy's possible

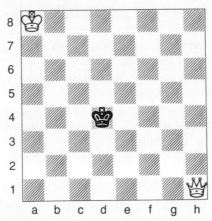

*Diagram 12.4*

moves, whatever he does to try to escape.

Here is one way this particular ending could go –

 **1 Qf3**

denying Black's King the 3rd rank and putting up a barrier down the f-file.

 **1 ... Ke5**
 **2 Kb7**

bringing the King nearer the scene of the action, since we cannot really improve the Queen's position.

 **2 ... Kd4**
 **3 Kb6 Ke5**
 **4 Kc5**

leaving only one square to which the black King can move, even though he is still in the centre!

 **4 ... Ke6**
 **5 Qf4 Ke7**
 **6 Qf5 Kd8**

the black King having been driven to the back row, where he can be forced to remain.

 **7 Qf7 Kc8**
 **8 Kb6 Kb8**
 **9 Qb7**

mate.

There is a slightly shorter method but this series of moves shows the general idea.

Did you notice that throughout the series of moves described there was no check at all until the final checkmating move? Some beginners think that to give check is all important and might have set about the position in diag. 12.4 like this –

 **1 Qd1+ Ke5**
 **2 Qe2+ Kd5**
 **3 Qd3+ Ke5**
 **4 Qb5+**

and the black King is still in the centre of the board, while the white King remains out of the action. So no real progress has been made towards checkmating the black King.

Do practise these endings. Sooner or later you will come across a situation where you will have to take care not to stalemate your opponent. Remember, your opponent may be hoping that you will fall for a stalemate trap – especially if you are in time trouble – so that he can 'steal' a draw from a game that *you* should have won.

It is not easy to spot all possible stalemate traps. It is impractical to give a *typical* example, since one player may think it too obvious, while another (quite good) player could be fooled by it. But try this:

*Diagram 12.5* Set up this position on your board and play these moves as quickly as possible. 1 Qe4 Kd8 2 Kb7 Kd7 3 Qe5 Kd8 4 Qe6 (Whoops!)

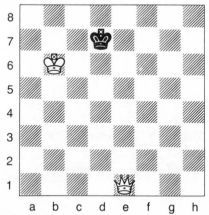

*Diagram 12.5*

## Solution

Diagram 12.3 There are a number of ways of checkmating from this diagram position. Here are just two –

    **1   Kb3+**

(you will have noticed that all three pieces were on the same diagonal in this case, so when the white King is moved the black King is exposed to a check from the Queen)

    **1   ...    Ke4**
    **2   Qf6!   Kd5**
    **3   Kc3    Ke4**

(desperately trying to stay in the centre of the board)

    **4   Kc4    Ke3**
    **5   Qf5    Ke2**

    **6   Qf4    Kd1**

(got him on the edge – now to keep him there)

    **7   Kd3    Ke1**
    **8   Qf8!**

(waiting)

    **8   ...    Kd1**
    **9   Qf1    mate.**

**or**

    **1   Qe1**

(immediately cutting off half of the board from the black King)

    **1   ...    Kd5**
    **2   Kc3    Kc5**
    **3   Qe5+**

(pushing the King further back)

    **3   ...    Kc6**
    **4   Kc4    Kb6**
    **5   Qd6+**

(and back)

    **5   ...    Kb7**
    **6   Kb5**

(and back)

    **6   ...    Kc8**
    **7   Qe7**

(*not*, whatever you do, **Kb6** or **Kc6** – stalemate)

    **7   ...    Kb8**
    **8   Kb6    Ka8**
    **9   Qe8    mate.**

\*      \*      \*

Castling was undoubtedly another result of efforts to speed up play. As the King needed protection early in a game, when the opponent had a full strength army with which to attack him, players used to spend a great deal of time moving the King into a corner of the board, behind a protective row of pawns. The centre pawns had usually been sent off into the battle, so the King was open to attack as long as he remained on his starting square.

But by moving him along the back rank towards a corner, the appropriate Rook was shut in, and it required a weakening of the defensive wall of pawns to let him out and into the fray.

As you will see in Unit 13, Castling provided a simple and effective method of achieving both ends. In one move the King is placed in some safety, while the Rook is brought nearer to the centre where he can begin to use his strength to attack or defend as required.

\*      \*      \*

# Unit 13

## Castling

This is the only time in a chess game when the King can move *two* squares in a single move. It is also the only occasion when *two* pieces are moved at the same time.

Castling involves the King and one of his Rooks and is carried out on either the King's side or the Queen's side as follows:

*On the King's side* – the King is moved two squares towards the King's Rook and is placed on the King's Knight's starting square. The Rook is then placed on the King's Bishop's square.

So if White were castling King's side, he would take his King from e1 and place it on g1. Then he would take his Rook from h1 and place it on f1.

*On the Queen's side* – the King is again moved two squares, but this time White's King would move from e1 to c1 and his Queen's Rook would move from a1 to d1.

The King or the Rook concerned *must not have been moved already* in the game – even if they have returned to their original starting squares.

The King *cannot* castle while he is in check.

The King cannot pass over squares that are attacked, nor can he land on a square that is attacked. In the first case he would be castling 'through' check, and in the second case he would be castling 'into' check – and as you know, a King cannot legally move into check.

The only other condition of castling is that the squares between the King and the Rook concerned must be clear, i.e. they must not be occupied by either your own pieces or those of your opponent.

The following series of diagrams will help you to understand castling.

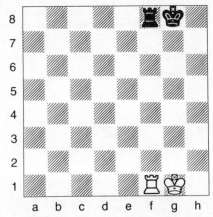

*Diagram 13.2    (After – King's side)*

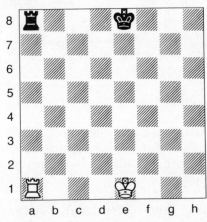

*Diagram 13.3    (Before – Queen's side)*

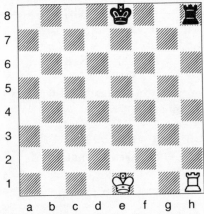

*Diagram 13.1    (Before – King's side)*

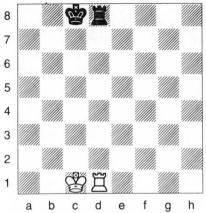

Diagram 13.4 *(After – Queen's side)*

Diagram 13.5 Set up this position on your board. It shows a number of the important features of castling. First note that White cannot castle at all, since his King is in check and it is not possible to castle out of check. So even though the squares between White's King and either Rook are clear, and assuming that the King and Rooks have *not* yet

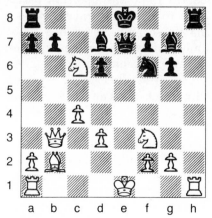

Diagram 13.5

been moved, he still cannot castle.

What are Black's castling possibilities? Can he castle on the King's side? Yes, Black can castle, assuming that neither his King nor the Rooks have been moved during the game.

Black's King's Rook is under attack from White's Rook on h1, but this would not stop Black from castling – since his King is not attacked by White's Rook, nor are the other squares concerned, f8 and g8.

Can Black castle on the Queen's side? No, because his King would have to cross over the d8 square which is controlled by White's Knight.

Do you think that Black could castle Queen's side if the white Knight were on b6? (Put it there.) From this square he is attacking the Rook but not the King. Well the answer is again *no* since the Knight is also attacking c8, and the King cannot move into check.

Diagram 13.6 Now set up this position. It is another one crowded with possibilities. Firstly, can White castle King's side? No. Black's Bishop on a7 is attacking g1, so the King is denied that square.

What about White's castling Queen's side? This is possible. Black's Bishop on f5 is attacking b1, but the King does not have to pass over or land on this square. The

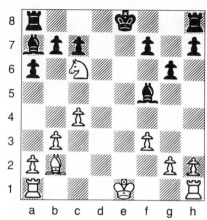

Diagram 13.6

Rook can, of course, always pass across squares that are attacked if he wishes to, like any other piece except the King.

Now Black. His King is not in check, but the white Bishop on b2 is attacking his Rook on h8. Does this matter with regard to castling? No, so Black could go ahead and castle King's side. What about castling Queen's side? Black could not do this. The Knight on c6 is attacking (among others) the square d8, and the King cannot pass over an attacked square.

Finally, one interesting possibility that can happen when castling is shown in diagrams 13.7 and 13.8. White to play, castles, and at the same time gives check to the black King.

This possibility doesn't occur often, but it can, and now you know about it.

In chess notation, castling King's

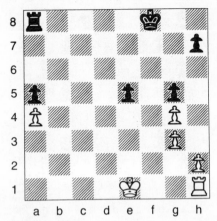

Diagram 13.7

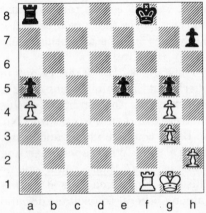

Diagram 13.8

side is shown as 0–0 and castling Queen's side is shown as 0–0–0.

Castling with check (as in diag. 13.8) would be written 0–0+, or if it had been Queen's side 0–0–0+.

Since you know the various ways the pieces can move it would be easy for you to read more into these diagrams than is intended, but do not worry about what could or could not

happen in the positions shown – we are only concerned with castling at the moment.

Of course you could see in diag. 13.5 that White would have to get out of check if it were his move, and since White is in check it cannot possibly be Black's move, can it?

In diag. 13.6, if it were Black to move, he would either castle King's side and save his Rook from the white Bishop attacking from b2, or move the Rook to g1 or f1 (which would mean that his chances of castling King's side later in the game would be gone). Alternatively he could capture the white Knight on c6 with his pawn on b7.

If it were White to move from the diagram position, he could, as we have said, castle Queen's side, or he could play 1 Nxa7, in which case Black, who could not afford to be a piece down, would probably recapture the Knight with his Rook from a8 (but then his Queen's side castling chances would be gone).

White could instead capture the black Rook on h8 'free of charge', since the capturing Bishop could not be retaken.

You will gather from the preceding comments that although a player cannot castle out of check or through check he *can* castle later, after the check has been broken either by interposing or by the capturing of the opponent's checking piece. He could not, of course, castle later if he had made the capture

with his King or had moved his King out of check. (Once the King or the Rook concerned has moved, castling cannot take place later in the game, as was mentioned earlier.)

When you castle depends entirely upon your own reading of a game or on your intentions. There is a useful expression which helps a lot. It is – 'Castle if you want to, or if you must, but *not* just because you can'.

\* \* \*

Although chess is played in many countries throughout the world, at the highest level the game has for many years been dominated by the Soviet Union.

While chess had been played in Russia before 1917, it was the October Revolution of that year which really saw the start of this dominance. The game was considered to be an important part of plans to bring cultural activities to the masses, who responded almost immediately by producing potential World Champions.

The first Russian-born World Champion was Alexander Alekhine, who won the title in 1927 from Jose Raoul Capablanca, a Cuban who had held the title since 1921. Alekhine defended his title in 1929 and 1934 against another Russian-born player, Efim Bogoljubow (who had taken German nationality in 1927) and on both occasions Alekhine retained his crown.

In 1935, a Dutchman, Dr Max Euwe, challenged and defeated Alekhine, but sportingly agreed to an early return match, and two years later Alekhine won back the title.

The 1939–1945 world war obviously disrupted international chess, and as Alekhine had died in 1946, FIDE (the World Chess Federation – see page iii) staged a match-tournament in 1948 for the vacant title. Botvinnik, Keres and Smyslov from the Soviet Union, Euwe from Holland, and Reshevsky from the United States played in the match. Reuben Fine, another American, was also invited but did not play.

Botvinnik won the match easily, three points ahead of Smyslov, and since then only Robert J. Fischer (USA) has disturbed the Russian domination of the world title:

1951 Botvinnik drew 12–all with Bronstein, thus retaining the crown.

1954 Botvinnik again drew 12–all, this time with Smyslov.

1957 Smyslov was successful, beating Botvinnik by 3 points.

1958 Botvinnik regained the title, beating Smyslov by 2 points.

1960 Tal beat Botvinnik by 4 points.

1961 Botvinnik again regained the title, winning easily by 5 points.

1963 Petrosian took the title, beating Botvinnik by 3 points.

1966 Petrosian held off Spassky by only one point.

1969 Spassky beat Petrosian by 2 points.

1972 At last came a break in the Russian monopoly of the World Chess Championship when Fischer beat Spassky, in a famous match in Reykjavik, Iceland, by 4 points.

1974 Back to the Soviet Union and an eliminating match between Anatoly Karpov and Victor Korchnoi to determine who should challenge Fischer. However, Fischer rejected the terms laid down for the challenge, and Karpov, having beaten Korchnoi in the eliminator, was declared World Champion.

1978 Korchnoi again fought his way through the preliminaries to a confrontation with Karpov, but this time the match was known in advance to be for the world crown.

The match was to be decided in favour of the first player to reach a total of 6 wins, and after 27 games Karpov led 5–2. It seemed to be all over, but Korchnoi, despite many gloomy predictions by the pundits, made a glorious comeback. He won Games 28 and 29, drew Game 30 and won Game 31.

Five–all and the match was poised in a nerve-stretching 'sudden-death' situation. The end came very suddenly indeed. In the very next game Korchnoi played badly – and lost – leaving a much-relieved Karpov still World Champion.

\*     \*     \*

# Unit 14

## Pieces in Action

Units 1 to 13 were designed to make sure that you fully understood the powers and limitations of each of the individual chess pieces.

If you have studied each Unit carefully and worked through the exercises properly, you will now be quite competent with the individual pieces. You must next learn one of the most important aspects of chess, which is that no matter how much power any of the pieces may have by itself it is vital to use it *in combination with* other pieces. Even the Queen needs help most of the time in order to realize her full powers.

Always remember that you should *never* start an attack until you can use *at least* two pieces together, and always try to base your defence on more than one piece.

So far, although we have had only a few pieces on the board at one time, there has been much to think about. When the board is full of pieces things are more complicated and it is more difficult to think about the right things in the right order.

'Have I left a piece where it can be captured for nothing?' (If so, another French expression is used to describe this – the piece is said to be 'en prise'.) 'Can I capture one of my opponent's pieces and get away with it?' 'Shall I exchange a certain piece, or shall I leave it where it is?' Gradually, we hope to show you how to direct your thoughts to those things that matter at the time. How to understand what is going on in various parts of the board. How to sum up a situation so you make fewer bad moves or errors and more good moves that will improve your position and/or weaken your opponent's. For the moment, we will not try to run before we can walk. Remember that up to now we have really only been crawling! You can't expect to learn all about chess in a short time, but as you learn more about each piece, each type of position, each part of the game, etc., the whole picture will become clearer – you will become better, win more games, increase your rate of improvement, and so on . . . If you have followed carefully and practised what we have shown you so far, you have a pretty good idea of the strengths and weaknesses of the pieces.

It is now time to give you a 'rough and ready' guide to the value of the pieces when compared with each other. We must stress that this is ONLY a guide and the value of the pieces can alter – sometimes quite a lot – depending upon the position on the board at the time.

If we take the pawn as worth one point, we can draw up a table of approximate values as follows:

MAJOR PIECES –
    QUEEN 9 points
    ROOK 5 points
MINOR PIECES –
    BISHOP 3 points
    KNIGHT 3 points

Use this table to help you in the early stages, but think of it as a crutch that can be thrown away once you are able to stand on your own feet and work out for yourself the value one piece would have in relation to another in a certain position. As you learn more about the game you will find that you are able to work these things out without seeming to think about it. Meanwhile, these values can be a guide when you have to exchange or try to win pieces.

Why is the King not on the list? Because he is a piece to which we obviously cannot give a value. Lose him and you have lost the game – he is 'priceless'. He is a special piece needing special treatment.

Consider diag. 14.1. Set up the position on your board so that you can make the moves as they are given and see their effects for yourself.

White can play 1 Nxe5, seeming to win a pawn, but after Black's reply 1 . . . Qd4! (attacking both the

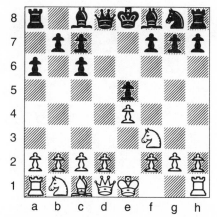

Diagram 14.1

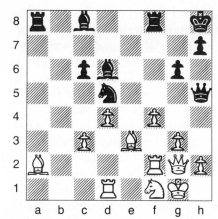

Diagram 14.2

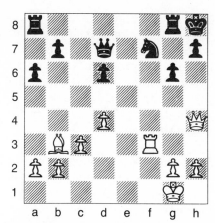

Diagram 14.3

Knight *and* the e-pawn) and 2 Nf3 Qxe4+, White must either put his King on f1 (blocking in his Rook) or exchange Queens by 3 Qe2 Qxe2+ 4 Kxe2, with hardly any chance of gaining an advantage.

So instead of capturing the pawn White should have castled, tucking his King away safely and bringing the Rook nearer the centre.

When most of the pieces have been removed from the board you can use your King more freely – and more safely. Indeed, we have seen how useful the King can be in the end game, and in many end games he is more than just useful – he is essential.

Let us now examine some more positions containing a large number of pieces with various possibilities of exchange or capture. Set up the diagram positions carefully on your board before reading

what we have to say about them.

*Diagram 14.2*   You are Black and it is your move. What do you do?

There is a choice of captures here. You may have thought of 1 ... Rxa2, but after White replies 2 Rxa2 you have lost a Rook for a Bishop – 5 points for 3, which makes you 2 points down according to our table of values. This is called losing the exchange.

What about 1 ... Nxe3? No. White replies 2 Nxe3, and you have merely exchanged a Knight for a Bishop – no loss in points value, but no gain either.

The best move is 1 ... Qxd1, which wins you the undefended Rook for nothing.

*Diagram 14.3*   What would you play for White here?

Counting up the pieces, we can see that you are a whole Rook down

with only a pawn to show for it. But both your Bishop and your Rook are attacking the Knight on f7, which is defended by only the Queen. Take advantage of this situation by playing either 1 Bxf7 or 1 Rxf7, and if the black Queen recaptures, *you* recapture with a considerable gain. Count up. You win a Knight and a Queen for the loss of a Bishop or a Rook.

The black Queen would, however, be reluctant to recapture on f7, since Black *is* a Rook for a pawn up and so the loss of the Knight could be accepted. But what if the Queen was forced to recapture? To achieve this you would have to play 1 Rxf7, attacking the black Queen, and if she moved away (rather than recapturing), 2 Qxh7 mate (or 2 Rxh7 mate if you prefer).

We hope that you did not decide to play 1 Qf6+ Rg7 2 Bxf7 Rf8!, since you would be in real trouble (work it out). Do *not* play a checking move just for the sake of it. You will no doubt, sooner or later, hear the ridiculous expression 'Never miss a check, it might be mate'. Consider the mess that that piece of advice would have got you into in the above situation.

*Diagram 14.4* What can White do here? There are plenty of 'good' moves, but we want to choose the best one.

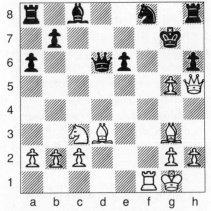

*Diagram 14.4*

What about 1 Bxd6, winning the Queen (9 points) for nothing? Surely we can't do better than this? But ... Black's King looks weak. Can we attack it in some way?

1 gxh6+ Rxh6 doesn't help, since if we play 2 Qxh6+, Black replies 2 ... Kxh6 and we have given up our Queen for only a Rook, with no obvious advantage to make this sacrifice worthwhile.

So let's try 1 Qg6+. It looks like mate because the black King can't move anywhere and he can't capture the Queen because White's Bishop on d3 is *guarding* her. But we have forgotten the Knight on f8. 1 Qg6+ fails to 1 ... Nxg6.

Where else can we look for a way to exploit the poorly defended black King? What about the f7 square? This is guarded only by the King himself, which is no protection at all, since we are attacking it twice! So 1 Rf7+. This is still not good enough, since the King can escape to g8. But 1 Qf7 *is* checkmate. The King cannot capture the Queen, since she is defended by the Rook on f1, and from f7 the Queen controls all Black's possible escape squares.

You probably spotted this mate quite early in our calculations but we tried the other lines of attack first to encourage you to look at *all* the possibilities before committing yourself to a move. There is a useful expression to remember: 'When you have found a good move, look for a better one.' Like all advice in chess this can have its drawbacks, but it is always a good idea to have a careful look around before making a move (just to make sure that there is nothing better).

*Diagram 14.5* What would you play for White here? This position looks quite complicated, but it should not take you long to see that it is the black Queen that is your

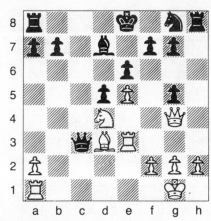

*Diagram 14.5*

main worry. Clearly you cannot allow Black to win a Rook for nothing by his playing 1 ... Qxa1+, so you must do something about defending or moving this Rook. Could you just move the Rook to, say, b1 or d1? To find out, let us examine the position in detail.

Although the black Queen is attacking your Bishop on d3, he is defended by the Rook on e3. What about the Knight on d4? Only your Queen is defending him. Unless you do something about it, Black can attack your Queen by playing ... Nh6 or ... Rh4 (supported by the pawn on g5) and your Knight on d4 is lost once his protective Queen is forced away.

If your Bishop were not on d3, your Rook on e3 would be attacking the black Queen, and, since it is your move, you could then capture her. But the Bishop *is* on d3, and if you simply moved him the black

Queen would just get herself away from the attack of the Rook on e3 and capture the Rook on a1 in the process. Really you need to move the Bishop with a check. This would force Black to do something about the check and then the Queen would be yours.

The trouble is that Black's own Bishop on d7 is stopping you giving check by moving your Bishop to b5, and his f-pawn is stopping 1 Bg6+. Could you lure the Bishop or the f-pawn away? You could play 1 Qxe6+, giving up your Queen for a pawn. Unthinkable! But is it unthinkable? 1 ... fxe6 2 Bg6+ Ke7 3 Rxc3, getting the Queen back and winning a pawn. If after your 'shock' move 1 Qxe6+, Black had replied 1 ... Ne7, blocking the check, you could have continued 2 Qxd7+ Kxd7 3 Bb5+!, and would still have got the Queen back.

But just as you are getting excited you realize that Black has another reply to your 1 Qxe6+. He could play 1 ... Bxe6! 2 Bb5+ Qc6! 3 Bxc6+ bxc6, and you would have given up a Bishop for only a pawn. If only that black pawn had been on b6 instead of b7. Ah well, chess is full of 'if only's'.

So have you wasted your time thinking about all those moves? Not at all. Until you checked them you could not know if there was a flaw in the combination, and it is good to use your imagination, even if the results are not always as rewarding as you would have hoped. Next time such a combination could well save the game for you – or better.

But let us go back to the original diagram position. A world champion was playing the white pieces and you may now understand why he continued with the 'quiet' move 1 Nb3! The Knight moves away from a possible attack from the black Queen (if the white Queen were driven away) defends the Rook on a1, frees his own Queen to attack Black's pawn on g5, and threatens moves like Rc1 and Bb5. So White has achieved a lot of things – generally improving his own position and weakening his opponent's – all with one 'quiet' move.

'Quiet' moves are very important in their proper place. We can get carried away by possible moves that provide lots of immediate action, but we must always be aware of what a 'quiet' move can achieve.

Now here are some positions for you to consider on your own. Set up each of these on your board and write down the moves you think best for both sides. Then, when you are satisfied that you have investigated the various possibilities, look at the solutions.

*Diagram 14.6* White to move. How can he gain most benefit from a series of exchanges on d5? (Be sure you get the right order of moves.)

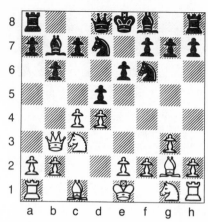

*Diagram 14.6*

*Diagram 14.7* If White plays 1 Bxc6, will he gain material?

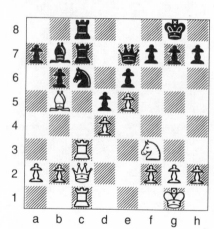

*Diagram 14.7*

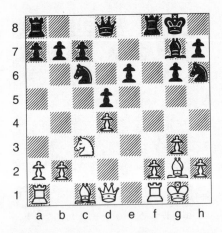

*Diagram 14.8* What would you play for Black here?

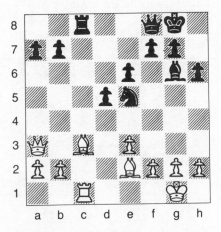

*Diagram 14.9* White to move. There are two possible captures – 1 Bxe5 or 1 Qxa7 – or an exchange – 1 Qxf8+. Examine each of these moves in turn and decide which is the best and why.

## Solutions

**Diagram 14.6** It often happens in chess that there are several pieces on both sides trained on one square. In such a situation you must count up all the possible exchanges and get the order right. Here the series of exchanges are as follows: 1 cxd5 exd5 2 Nxd5 Nxd5 3 Bxd5 Bxd5, 4 Qxd5, and White has won a pawn. Notice two things. Firstly, if the moves had been 2 Bxd5 Nxd5 3 Nxd5, Black would still have lost the pawn but his Bishop on b7 could prove very strong down the long white-square diagonal. Secondly, if White had wrongly captured with his Queen on move 3, Black could have replied 3 ... Bxd5, winning the Queen for a Bishop. So the best order of moves is *when there is a steady increase in the value of the pieces captured.*

**Diagram 14.7** No, White cannot gain material because after 1 Bxc6 Bxc6 2 Rxc6 Rxc6 3 Qxc6 Rxc6 4 Rxc6, he ends up with the last piece on c6, he has gained two Rooks, a Bishop and a Knight (5+5+3+3=16 points) but has lost a Bishop, a Rook and a Queen (3+5+9=17 points).

Now look at the difference if White's Rook on c1 had been on c2 and his Queen had been on c1. Then, White would have made a profit.

**Diagram 14.8** White has a very weak pawn on d4, defended only by the Queen while attacked by Black's Knight (on c6) and Bishop (on g7). It looks easy for Black, since after 1 ... Nxd4 2 Qxd4? Bxd4 3 Bxh6, he has gained a Queen and a pawn (10 points) for the loss of two Knights (6 points). However, let us play it another way for White: 1 ... Nxd4 2 Bxh6! Bxh6 3 Qxd4, and it is White who has won the exchanges, gaining two Knights (6 points) for a Bishop and a pawn (4 points). So Black's best first move is 1 ... Nf5!, after which there is nothing White can do to save his d-pawn.

**Diagram 14.9** It is clearly wrong to play 1 Bxe5, since Black could reply 1 ... Rxc1+.

1 Qxa7 looks good, since it wins a pawn – and even two if Black replies 1 ... Ra8 2 Qxb7 (3 ... Rxa2? 3 Bxe5, and things get even worse for Black).

However, 1 Qxf8+! is best, because 1 ... Rxf8 allows 2 Bxe5, winning the Knight for nothing, and 1 ... Kxf8 fails to 2 Bb4+, since the King must move and White can follow up with 3 Rxc8+, winning a Rook.

# Unit 15

## The Double Attack – With the Pawn and with the Knight

Chess would, of course, be easy if your opponent just left pieces lying around to be captured, but normally you have to use your skill to win material. The 'Double Attack' means exactly what it says: you play a move that threatens two enemy pieces at the same time, so that if one moves away you can win the other – always provided that your attacking piece is suitably supported where necessary.

The following diagrams and comments illustrate this type of

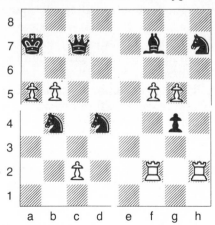

*Diagram 15.1*

attack. First we deal with the double attack by the pawn.

*Diagram 15.1 (top left)* White plays 1 b6+, attacking both the King and the Queen. Even if the Queen captured the attacking pawn, the other pawn – on a5 – would recapture her. Black's King would then take this second pawn, but to lose a Queen for two pawns is a tremendous blow, and unless there were some compensation elsewhere in the position Black would have given up the game here. *(top right)* The same sort of situation here, except that Black at least has a choice as to which of the two attacked pieces he wishes to retain. After White plays 1 g6, Black is not forced to play 1 . . . Bxg6, in which case White would reply 2 fxg6 and the Knight would move away. Black could reply 1 . . . Bg8 and capture White's pawn after it had taken the Knight on h7.
*(bottom left)* White plays 1 c3 and one of the Knights is doomed, though 1 c3 Nbc2 2 cxd4 Nxd4 at least wins back the pawn as some consolation for Black.
*(bottom right)* A black pawn is about to attack two white Rooks by moving to g3. White can, of course, move only one of them – and he would presumably move it somewhere along the rank, so that he can at least recapture the pawn.

Now for an opening trap showing a double attack by a pawn as early as move 7 in a game. The opening is an example of 'Alekhine's Defence' and shows one of the rare occasions when it is necessary for a player to move the same piece twice in the opening, rather than use the moves to develop other pieces.

| 1 | e4 | Nf6 |
|---|-----|------|
| 2 | e5 | Nd5 |
| 3 | d4 | d6 |
| 4 | Nf3 | Nc6 |
| 5 | e6!? | |

(a very good *or* a risky move, depending upon what Black replies)

| 5 | . . . | Bxe6? |
|---|-------|-------|

(he chose the wrong reply)

| 6 | c4 | Nb6 |
|---|-----|------|
| 7 | d5 | |

– a double attack – and Black must lose a piece. Black of course gains two pawns for it but is still the equivalent of a pawn down.

Black would have avoided this double attack if he had captured the original pawn on his fifth move by playing 5 . . . fxe6, instead of taking with the Bishop.

The Knight uses the double attack probably more than any other piece except the Queen. A double attack by the Knight is called 'a fork', because it is an obvious 'two-pronged' attack, and it is really exciting (as well as deadly) to play. Here are some examples.

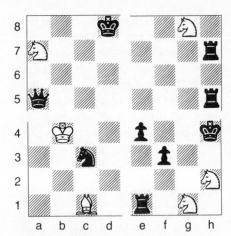

*Diagram 15.2*

*Diagram 15.2 (top left)* White plays 1 Nc6+ and forks the King and the Queen. The King is forced to move out of check, so the Queen is lost, and with no compensation. Before we leave this diagram, reverse the position of the King and the Knight. Now play 1 Nc6+. Here Black can move his King to a square next to the Queen (a6 or b6), so that after the Knight captures the Queen the King can at least recapture the Knight, gaining some small compensation for Black. In an actual game the loss of the Queen – even for a minor piece – would be too much to bear unless there were some other compensation for the player whose Queen had been captured.

*(top right)* White plays 1 Nf6 and all Black can do is choose the square upon which the capture of one of his Rooks will take place. Obviously Black will move one of the Rooks along the file so that he can recapture the Knight. In an actual game it may be quite important which square his remaining Rook occupies after he has lost the exchange.

*(bottom left)* The straightforward Knight fork is probably becoming obvious to you by now, and you will see that if Black played 1 . . . Na2+, he would win White's Bishop for nothing.

*(bottom right)* Just a little more complicated – two Knights this time. White is obviously going to gain two pawns and a Rook for the loss of one of his Knights.

White's first move is to capture the pawn on f3 with a check using either of his Knights. Black replies 1 . . . exf3, but White's other Knight then recaptures again with a check and wins the Rook, since Black is forced to move his King.

Note that if the Rook had been on h2 and the Knights on e1 and g1, Black would have gained both Knights for the loss of the two pawns and the Rook.

Here is a short game showing the Knight fork at work. (It was played by co-author John Littlewood, as a youngster, in his first County Match.) Set up the board and play through the moves.

The opening is a King's Gambit Declined, and John played White.

| 1 | e4 | e5 |
|---|-----|------|
| 2 | f4 | Nc6 |
| 3 | Nf3 | exf4 |
| 4 | d4 | d5 |
| 5 | exd5 | Qxd5 |
| 6 | Nc3 | Qd6? |

(6 . . . Bb4, is better)

| 7 | d5 | Nce7 |
|---|-----|------|
| 8 | Nb5! | Qc5 |

(8 . . . Qxd5? would have allowed 9 Nxc7+, forking the King, Queen and Rook)

| 9 | Bxf4 | Nxd5 |
|----|------|------|
| 10 | Qxd5! | Qb4+ |

(desperation, since Black sees that he would lose a piece to the same Knight fork after 10 . . . Qxd5 11 Nxc7+ etc.)

| 11 | Qd2 | Qxb2 |
|----|------|------|
| 12 | Nxc7+ | |

(forking the King and the Rook)

| 12 | . . . | Ke7 . |
|----|-------|-------|

Now if you would have played 13 Nxa8, winning a Rook, go to the bottom of the class. Why? Well, look instead at 13 Qd6. (!)

One thing that became obvious in this game was that the *threat* of a Knight fork forced Black to make some bad moves. This is a lesson to remember. In chess the threat is often much more effective than the execution.

Here are some positions that arose from actual play where a Knight fork sooner or later proved deadly. See if you can find the right moves. Set up each of the positions on your board and write down the moves before you look at the solutions.

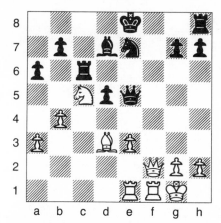

*Diagram 15.3*

*Diagram 15.3* Momo – McGovan (Moscow 1956). White to move. 1 Qf7+ Kd8 would not be useful, but White has a Knight fork in mind by which he can win a piece.

*Diagram 15.4* Pirc – Byrne (1932). This time it is Black to move first. He sees the chance of a Knight fork, but still has to 'set it up'. He starts 1 . . . Rxc3+! and White

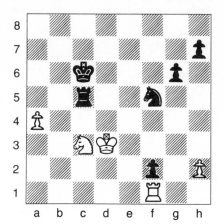

*Diagram 15.4*

replies 2 Kxc3, Black giving up the exchange – a Rook for a Knight. He must have something pretty powerful in mind. What do you think he is after?

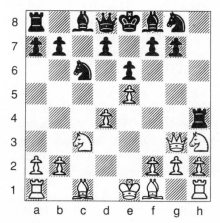

*Diagram 15.5*

*Diagram 15.5* Frey – Katz (Geneva 1956). Black plays 1 . . . Nxd4, threatening the double attack by . . . Nc2+. This looks like a mistake after White plays 2 Bg5, attacking the Queen and Rook, but Black replies 2 . . . Rxh3! White plays 3 gxh3, and at this stage Black has gained a pawn and a Knight (total 4 points) for the loss of a Rook (5 points). After his next three moves, though, Black is two points up on this combination. How does he achieve this two point advantage?

*Diagram 15.6* Matulovic – Zvet-kov (Varna 1965). Black wrongly

plays 1 . . . Qxe5?, failing to see White's plan. Imagine you are White and find his moves from here

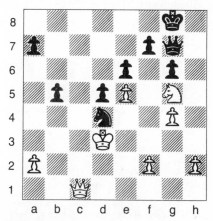

*Diagram 15.6*

on. A clue – at the end of this combination Black's Knight is trapped, still on d4!

*Diagram 15.7* Petrosian – Simagin (Moscow 1956). White to move. He cannot play Nxf7 because if Black replied 1 . . . Qd1+ White would be unable to escape the

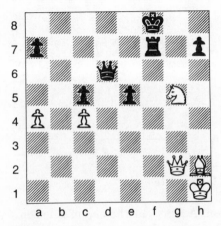

*Diagram 15.7*

checks. Try it for yourself. This type of situation is called 'perpetual check' and can obviously only result in a drawn game. White therefore plays 1 Qa8+ and Black replies 1 . . . Kg7. Then . . . ? (Be careful, it's not as easy as it looks.)

## Solutions

**Diagram 15.3** White begins by giving up his Queen 1 Qf8+!, but then 1 . . . Rxf8 2 Rxf8+ Kxf8 3 Nxd7+ Black has to move his King 4 Nxe5, and White comes out of it a piece up.

**Diagram 15.4** After 1 . . . Rxc3+!

2 Kxc3 Ne3!, the white Rook must take the pawn or it will Queen next move. But of course 3 Rxf2 allows 3 . . . Nd1+, winning the Rook for Black. Note that if there were no white pawn on h2, Black could have played 2 . . . Ng3 3 Rxf2 Ne4+, again forking the King and Rook. So Black did not lose the exchange after all. He ended up winning the Knight for nothing.

**Diagram 15.5** After 1 . . . Nxd4 2 Bg5 Rxh3! 3 gxh3 Qxg5! 4 Qxg5 Nf3+, White's King and Queen are forked, so Black comes out ahead with a Knight, a Bishop and a pawn for a Rook.

**Diagram 15.6** White won by 2 Qc8+ Kg7 3 Qh8+! Kxh8 4 Nxf7+ followed by 5 Nxe5, when the final clever point is seen – Black's Knight is trapped!

**Diagram 15.7** After 1 Qa8+ Kg7, if White plays 2 Qh8+, Black can reply 2 . . . Kg6! So 2 Bxe5+ Qxe5 and *then* 3 Qh8+! forces 3 . . . Kxh8, (or 4 Qxe5 wins the Black Queen) so that 4 Nxf7+ forks the King and the Queen.

# Unit 16

## The Double Attack – With the Bishop and with the Rook

We start with four examples of the double attack by the Bishop.

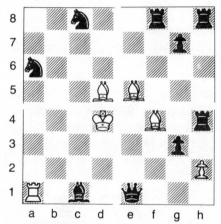

*Diagram 16.1*

*Diagram 16.1 (top left)* White plays 1 Bb7, attacking both Knights at the same time. They cannot defend each other in one move, so one of the Knights is lost for nothing.

*(top right)* White's Bishop takes the pawn on g7 and threatens both Rooks. He must win one of them. If in an actual game the Bishop were retaken on the next move, this would still be a good exchange for White, especially as he had won a pawn while getting into the position of attacking both Rooks.

*(bottom left)* Black checks the white King by playing Bb2+, and at the same time attacks the white Rook on a1. When the King moves out of check, Bxa1 gives Black the Rook for nothing.

*(bottom right)* White plays Bxg3, attacking the Queen and the Rook. The Queen could capture the Bishop, of course, but she would then be recaptured by the white pawn on h2. Black's best move would be to play 1 . . . Qe4. Then, after the Bishop has captured the Rook, the Queen can recapture the Bishop.

Now let us look at an example from an actual chess game.

*Diagram 16.2* The white Knight

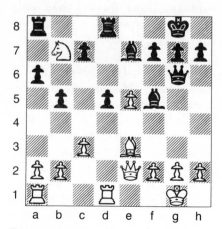

*Diagram 16.2*

is attacking the Rook on d8. Has Black anything better than to move the Rook out of the Knight's reach? Yes. He plays 1 . . . d4! 2 cxd4 Be4! Black now threatens, with a double attack by the Bishop, not only the Knight (on b7) but – much more important – checkmate on g2 by the Queen! If, after 1 . . . d4!, White had played 2 Nxd8 dxe3 3 Nb7, then once again 4 . . . Be4 wins the Knight, which, added to the Bishop won on e3, gives a net profit on the transaction to Black.

If you have been unable to solve the problems set for you up to now, do not worry. You will suddenly find that things are not as complicated as they seem. Take heart from the fact that even grandmasters can – and do – overlook even very simple ideas. Take this next situation, for example. Here a future world champion misses a simple idea.

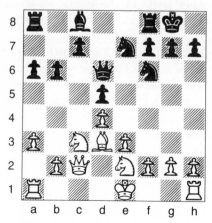

*Diagram 16.3*

**Diagram 16.3** Euwe – Alekhine (Zurich 1934). In the actual game Euwe played 1 b4, when he could have played — ? Well, what could he have played? See if you can spot what a potential world champion completely missed. Here are three clues: (i) remember that we are talking about the double attack by the Bishop; (ii) in the diagram position (which you should by now have set up on your board) Black's h-pawn is guarded by the Knight on f6; and (iii) if h7 is one target in our white-square Bishop's double attack plans, what else does Black have on a white square (unguarded) that the white Bishop could threaten at the same time?

The double attack by the Rook is often best seen in the end game, when the Rook is the ideal piece for picking up loose pawns. But this major piece is also very useful in other parts of the game, when he can pick up pieces as well as pawns.

**Diagram 16.4** (top left) Black plays 1 . . . Rxa6, and will win one of the Bishops as well as the pawn. (top right) 1 Rg6+ Qxg6 2 hxg6, gaining the Queen for the loss of a Rook – a good exchange for White. (bottom left) White plays 1 Rb2, and Black will lose a Knight. (bottom right) This shows an unusual but very important use of the double attack. With 1 . . . Re3, Black threatens not only the Bishop

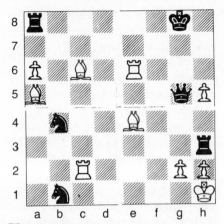

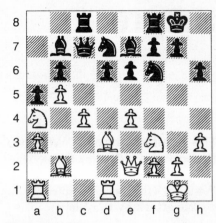

Diagram 16.4

Diagram 16.5

but also mate on e1. White must, of course, prevent the mate, so the Bishop is lost. (White stops the mating threat by making an 'escape hole' for his King. He would move one of his pawns forward to achieve this.)

Here are two examples from actual play, showing how to use a double attack by the Rook to advantage. Don't forget, that 'only' winning a pawn is a worthwhile advantage.

**Diagram 16.5** Najdorf – Reshevsky (Match 1952). Black won a useful pawn by the following combination: 1 . . . Bxe4! 2 Bxe4 Qxc4 3 Qxc4 Rxc4. Now Black wins back the piece he gave up for the pawn on move 1 because the Knight on a4 and the Bishop on e4 are both attacked and cannot both be defended. After 4 Nxb6 Rxe4, Black had won a useful pawn.

Now try to solve the next problem.

**Diagram 16.6** Schmid – Evans (Olympiad 1958). White spoils a good position by playing 1 f4?, completely missing Black's reply. Can you find what White missed and Black saw?

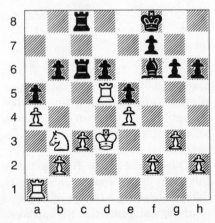

Diagram 16.6

## Solutions

Diagram 16.3  By playing 1 e4!
(threatening e5 next move, forking
the Queen and the Knight), White
forces Black to reply 1 . . . dxe4.
Now White can play 2 Nxe4, which
attacks the Queen and the Knight.
Black now has to lose the Knight's
protection of the h7 square, since if
he moved the Queen out of the way
White would play 3 Nxf6+. So
Black plays 2 . . . Nxe4, which
although it removes the protection
of h7 is probably his best move.
White next plays 3 Bxe4, which
attacks the Rook on a1 as well as
the pawn on h7. Naturally Black
does not want to lose the Rook, but
he must lose something. 3 . . . Bb7
loses that Bishop for nothing –
slightly less important than losing
a Rook, but still a piece down.
Alternatively he could move the
Rook (to b8 or a7) or his pawn from
c7 to c6. But whichever of these
moves Black chooses, White wins
the h-pawn by playing 4 Bxh7+.
The King cannot recapture, since
the Bishop is supported by the
Queen on c2, so Black is forced to
play 4 . . . Kh8.

So White wins a pawn, weakens
Black's defences around his King
and forces the King to make a
'nothing' move. White must not,
however, leave his Bishop on h7,
since if Black moved his g-pawn to
g6 the Bishop would be trapped, and
although White could play Bxg6,
Black would recapture with his
f-pawn or his Knight.

Diagram 16.6  After White played
1 f4?, Black replied 1 . . . exf4. Then
follows 2 gxf4 Bxc3 3 bxc3 Rxc3+
4 Kd2 Rxb3, and although White
gets one pawn back by 5 Rxd6, he
has a losing end game.

You may well have not spotted
this at your stage of chess development, since Black is 'only' a pawn
up and with both pairs of Rooks still
on the board you could have
thought that there was still a lot of
play left for both sides. Black has
considerable strength, however, if
he plays the end game correctly.

As you make progress and practise your end-game play you will
begin to appreciate the strengths
and weaknesses of positions when
there are still a number of pieces on
the board with what may appear to
be a fairly even division of strength.

Why not take this particular
game on from here. Take the Black
pieces and see if you can prove us
right – that White has 'a losing end
game'. Or take the White pieces and
try to prove us wrong. It will give
you excellent practice.

# Unit 17

## The Double Attack – With the Queen and with the King

As the Queen combines the powers of the Bishop *and* the Rook, she can mount some quite deadly double attacks.

*Diagram 17.1* (*top*) Here the Queen makes her double attack by moving along the rank from a5 to e5, where she can check the King on b8 and attack the Rook at the same time, so the Rook is lost.

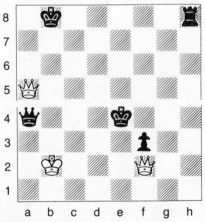

*Diagram 17.1*

(*bottom*) This shows an interesting application of the double attack.

Black plays 1 ... Qd4+, simply to force the exchange of Queens. After the exchange his pawn cannot be stopped, and its promotion would give Black a Queen to replace the one he exchanged.

Now look at this opening trap (agreed it is made possible because of Black's very bad play), which shows the Queen using a double attack to win a very important piece. Set up the pieces on your board to start a game.

| 1 | e4 | e5 |
| 2 | Nf3 | f6? |
| 3 | Nxe5! | fxe5? |
| 4 | Qh5+ | g6 |
| 5 | Qxe5+ | |

and however Black chooses to get out of this check White wins the Rook.

Now set up on your board the position shown in diagram 17.2, which is the one after White had

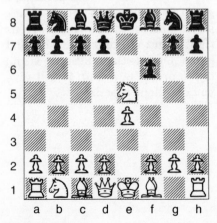

*Diagram 17.2*

played 3 Nxe5! in the above opening.

If instead of taking the Knight on move 3 Black had played 3 ... Qe7, and if play had continued 4 Qh5+ g6 5 Nxg6, Black would himself have had the opportunity of mounting a double attack by playing 5 ... Qxe4+ (see diag. 17.3) forcing White to get out of the check and allowing Black to play 6 ... Qxg6.

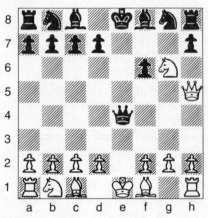

*Diagram 17.3*

You may have thought that in the opening trap Black could have avoided losing the Rook had he not played his g-pawn on move 4 to block the check from White's Queen. Well let's examine this further. Set up the position shown in diagram 17.4, which is that after White had played 4 ... Qh5+.

Instead of playing 4 ... g6, Black could have moved his King 4 ... Ke7. Unfortunately it doesn't help though, for after a series of

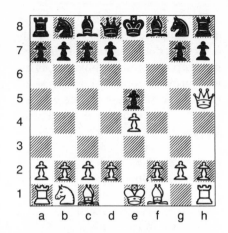

*Diagram 17.4*

checks Black is mated.

> 5　Qxe5+　Kf7
> 6　Bc4+　　Kg6
> 7　Qf5+　　Kh6
> 8　d4+

(from the Bishop on c1)

> 8　...　　　g5
> 9　h4!　　　Be7
> 10　hxg5+　Kg7
> 11　Qf7　　mate.

Now set up the position shown in diagram 17.5, which is that after White had played 6 Bc4+.

If Black had tried

> 6　...　　　d5

then after

> 7　Bxd5+　Kg6
> 8　h4　　　h6

White has

> 9　Bxb7!　Bxb7

clearing the way for

> 10　Qf5　　mate.

So whatever he tries after his terrible second and third moves,

Black has no way out. Losing a Rook is bad enough but being checkmated is much worse!

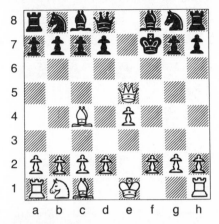

*Diagram 17.5*

Now for a very clever example from master play.

*Diagram 17.6* Boleslavsky – Flohr (Budapest 1950). White first plays 1 Qd3!, threatening Qxh7 mate and so forcing Black to play

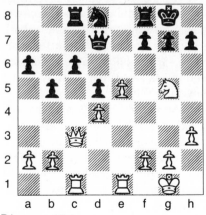

*Diagram 17.6*

1 ... g6 to stop it. (You will see in a moment why White was happy to force this move.) White then plays 2 Qa3!, with a double threat. Can you see it?

One half of the double threat is obvious – the Queen is attacking Black's undefended a-pawn – but it is not so easy to see that White is also threatening to play Nxh7!, since the Rook on f8 would be left undefended if Black retook the Knight by playing ... Kxh7.

You may think that instead of capturing the Knight (if it did take the h-pawn) Black should move his Rook away to e8, but if the Knight is not captured his next move would be to f6 with a check, forking the King and the Queen. Indeed, if Black did move the Rook to e8, White's Nf6+ would be attacking the King, the Queen *and* the Rook – a 'family fork'. So now the whole point of White's first move, Qd3, becomes clear. He wanted to remove the guard from f6, which he did by threatening mate and forcing Black's g-pawn to move from g7. All clear? If not, play it through again. This was a splendid piece of play by grand master Boleslavsky and was based upon the double attack.

Black could, of course, stop this major threat by playing 2 ... Ne6. Then the Rook would be defended, so Nxh7 Kxh7 would no longer be a good idea for White. But White would still win the a-pawn, thanks to the original double attack, since after 2 ... Ne6, 3 Nxe6, and however Black recaptured, 4 Qxa6 would win the pawn.

Now see if you can solve this position.

*Diagram 17.7* Tchigorin – Janowski (Paris 1900). White to move. A clue – it all starts with a double attack by the pawn. You probably spotted that anyway. A second clue – it would be useful if White could get his Queen to f8. Another double attack, on move 2, could help, since Black would have to lose a piece to avoid being checkmated. Right, off you go.

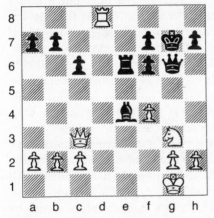

*Diagram 17.7*

By now you should have a healthy respect for double attacks and double-attack threats. We have seen how all the pieces can make various kinds of double attack, except the King. Some examples of double attacks by the King follow.

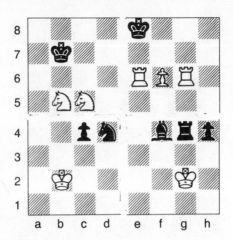

*Diagram 17.8*

*Diagram 17.8 (top left)* Here the black King is in check from the Knight on c5, but he can win one of the Knights by moving to either b6 or c6, since the Knights cannot guard each other in one move from such a position.

*(top right)* An amusing situation: after Black has played 1 ... Kf7, attacking both Rooks, White must wish that he did not have the pawn, since it is stopping his Rooks – both attacked by the King after this move – from defending each other.

*(bottom left)* 1 Kc3 will win the pawn for White.

*(bottom right)* 1 Kf3 attacks the Rook and the Bishop, neither of which can protect the other. Obviously since the Rook is the more valuable piece, Black will move it away along the file and give up the Bishop.

Here is an example of an uncommon (and very clever) use of the King in a double attack. This opening trap is not at all obvious, but it will provide a useful exercise for you to see whether or not you can spot it. Set up your pieces to start a game.

| 1 | e4 | e5 |
|---|------|------|
| 2 | Nf3 | Nc6 |
| 3 | Bb5 | a6 |
| 4 | Ba4 | d6 |
| 5 | Bxc6+ | bxc6 |
| 6 | d4 | f6 |
| 7 | Be3 | Ne7 |
| 8 | Nc3 | Rb8 |

Now, instead of protecting the pawn on b2, White plays

9 Qd2.

Can you see what White intends if Black now plays 9 ... Rxb2? You can give yourself a hearty pat on the back if you do!

## Solutions

Diagram 17.7   White plays 1 f5!, Black replies 1 . . . Bxf5, and White has prepared the double attack on the black Bishop and the f8 square. (Don't forget that squares can be attacked as well as pieces!) After 2 Qc5!, White is threatening the Bishop as well as Qf8 mate, so the Bishop is lost.

Diagram 17.9   After
  9   . . .   Rxb2?
White has
  10  dxe5   fxe5
  11  Nxe5!
and this Knight cannot be captured because if
  11  . . .   dxe5?
  12  Qxd8+ Kxd8
and White has the beautiful
  13  0–0–0+

winning the Rook. A clever double attack brought about in the process of castling.

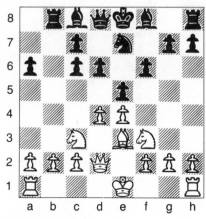

*Diagram 17.9*

# Unit 18

## More about Pawn Endings

Have you remembered everything you learned about pawn endings in Unit 8? Let us see if you have remembered at least two of the basic ideas.

*Diagram 18.1* You are playing the black pieces and have reached a position where, although White has the pawn, you can hold out and gain a draw. But everything depends upon your next move. What do you play, and why?

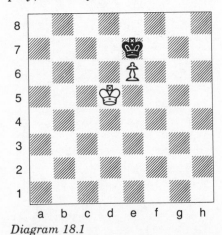

*Diagram 18.1*

*Diagram 18.2* Here you are White and it is your move. There is an easy

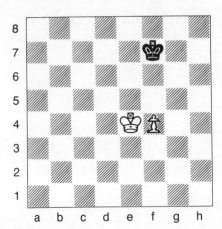

*Diagram 18.2*

win for you if you play the best move. What is it, and how would you go on to promote your pawn?

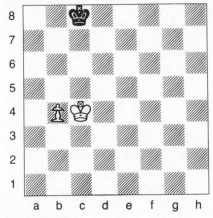

*Diagram 18.3*

*Diagram 18.3* Here is an interesting and instructive end-game position. It arose in a game between the experienced Yugoslav grand master Svetozar Gligoric and a 16 year-old player who was destined to

become world champion, Bobby Fischer. Gligoric, playing White, has the pawn, so the best young Fischer can hope for is a draw. The move he makes now is vital. He can move his King to any one of five squares, but only one of them is the right square.

It is *not*

| 1 | ... | Kb7? |

since

| 2 | Kb5! | Ka7 |
| 3 | Kc6 | Kb8 |
| 4 | b5 | Kc8 |
| 5 | b6 | Kb8 |
| 6 | b7 | Ka7 |
| 7 | Kc7 | |

and the pawn will promote.

Nor is it

| 1 | ... | Kc7? |
| 2 | Kc5! | Kb7 |
| 3 | Kb5! | Kc7 |
| 4 | Ka6 | |

etc. What about

| 1 | ... | Kd7? |

Again wrong:

| 2 | Kb5! | Kc8 |
| 3 | Ka6 | Kb8 |
| 4 | b5 | Ka8 |
| 5 | b6 | Kb8 |
| 6 | b7 | Kc7 |
| 7 | Ka7 | |

etc.

To Fischer the correct move 1 ... Kb8! was simply a 'matter of technique', but only because he had worked hard at endings when he was even younger! Why is it that this move will lead to a draw? To explain, we must introduce a new chess term – the *opposition*. If White replies 2 Kb5, Black 'takes the opposition' by playing 2 . . . Kb7!, that is by placing his King on the same file as the opposing King with one square between them. After this move Black 'has the opposition' because it is White to play. White would really prefer not to move, but the laws of chess force him to do so. If White plays 3 Kc5, Black replies . . . Kc7!, keeping the opposition and forcing a draw, since White can make no further progress without advancing the pawn. For example, 4 b5 Kb7 5 b6 Kb8! draws, as you know.

Go back to diag. 18.3 and look at the position of the Kings. Strangely enough it is White who has the 'distant opposition', that is his King is on the same file as the opposing King with an *odd* number of squares (in this case, 3) between them, and with Black to move. If White's pawn had been on b3 instead of b4, giving White the chance of a 'waiting move' with the pawn, 1 . . . Kb8 would *not* have saved Black. White would have replied 2 Kb4!, keeping the distant opposition, and play would have continued 2 . . . Kc8! (a good try) 3 Ka5! Kb8 4 Kb6!, and White would have forced a win as was shown in Unit 8.

White's pawn *is* on b4, however, preventing White from keeping the distant opposition. This means that after 1 . . . Kb8!, whatever White

does Black can take the opposition or bring his King up to the pawn. For example 2 Kd4 Kb7! 3 Kc5 Kc7! draws.

*Diagram 18.4* Let us now look at the opposition at work in this ending. Before you read on, however, try to promote the pawn against a friend. Then try to defend the position against the threatening promotion. In this way you will learn much more than by trying to memorize the lines of the play that follow.

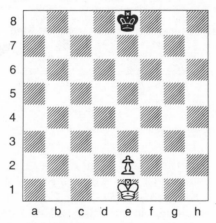

*Diagram 18.4*

All the play depends upon the opposition, as we shall see. Let us consider play with White to move first. 1 Kd2! (White must *not* move the pawn for reasons that will become clear later) 1 . . . Kd8! (taking the distant opposition, this time five squares away. (Remember that the opposition involves the Kings

having an odd number of squares between them.) Another way to remember this is that both Kings will be on squares of the same colour) 2 Ke3 Ke7! 3 Kd4 Kd6! 4 Ke4 Ke6! Black has done very well – he has done the best he could and has kept the opposition. But White has a move in reserve, 5 e3!, and this will win the game for him, since the black King must now give ground, leading to positions that we know well.

With Black to move first there is a big difference, because after 1 . . . Ke7! 2 Kd2 Kd6! 3 Ke3 Ke5!, Black has the opposition and White has no reserve pawn move with which to take over the opposition. Play might continue: 4 Kf3 Kf5 5 e3 Ke5 6 e4 Ke6 7 Kf4 Kf6, etc., and Black forces a draw!

If you have mastered the above position, you need never worry about playing a King and pawn versus King ending – whichever side you are on.

*Diagram 18.5* Here, if White has the move, he will clearly win by playing 1 h6, after which the pawn cannot be stopped (1 . . . Ke5 2 h7 Kf6 3 h8=Q+), while if Black has the move, 1 . . . Ke5 draws, since the King catches the pawn in time.

If you have any difficulty working out this sort of position – i.e. whether a King can catch an opposing pawn – it is a good idea to picture a large square, such as that drawn on the diagram. Unless the

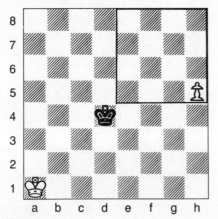

*Diagram 18.5*

King can immediately enter the square, he cannot stop the pawn from promoting. Knowing this, consider the following position?

*Diagram 18.6* White to move. What will be the result? Does our advice hold good here?

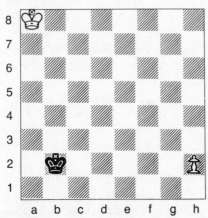

*Diagram 18.6*

Finally, an interesting position for you to consider.

*Diagram 18.7* White to move. What will be the result? Play this ending against a friend – a few times, if necessary.

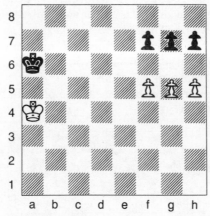

*Diagram 18.7*

## Solutions

Diagram 18.1 Only 1 . . . Ke8! draws. (2 Kd6 Kd8! 3 e7+ Ke8 4 Ke6 stalemate), 1 . . . Kd8?, for example, loses after 2 Kd6 Ke8 3 e7 Kf7 4 Kd7, etc, since the pawn can promote.

Diagram 18.2 Kf5! decides the game since Black must give way, for example 1 . . . Ke7 2 Kg6 Ke8! 3 Kg7 Ke7 4 f5, and White can go on to promote his pawn. However 1 f5? Kf6 or 1 Ke5? Ke7 would allow Black to draw. (See Unit 8.)

Diagram 18.6 White will win by playing 1 h4, after which the black King cannot catch the pawn before it promotes. You had probably guessed that this was a trick question. If you want to 'picture the square' in this case you have to imagine that the pawn is on h3! You must remember that the pawn can move *two* squares on his first move! With White to move first here, the black King would need to be on c3 to catch the pawn.

Diagram 18.7 White will win, but there is only one way for him to do so. He must play 1 g6!, giving a choice of two variations: (a) 1 . . . hxg6 2 f6! gxf6 3 h6, and the h-pawn is through; or (b) 1 . . . fxg6 2 h6! gxh6 3 f6, with a similar result.

Be careful about imitating this in *any* position. It works only here because White's pawns are far advanced and because the black King is not able to stop the nearest pawn. For example, with Black's King on c5 the plan would fail after 1 g6 fxg6! 2 h6 gxh6 3 f6 Kd6!, and it is Black who would win!

# Unit 19

## The Power of the Pin

The *pin* is really another form of the double attack, as the following examples will show.

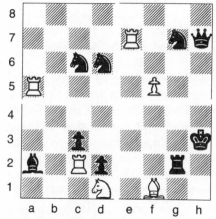

*Diagram 19.1*

*Diagram 19.1 (top left)* By playing 1 Ra6, White attacks the Knight on c6, but is ready to capture the other Knight (on d6) if the first Knight moves away. This is a kind of double attack, the Rook attacking one Knight 'through' the other. We say that the Knight on c6 is 'pinned'.

*(top right)* Here is a real pin – when a piece of higher value is caught behind a piece of lower value. In this case the Knight cannot move away or the Rook would capture the Queen. So White would play f6, and the Knight would be lost.

*(bottom left)* Here Black would play 1 Bb3, attacking the Rook and pinning it to the Knight. This version of the pin is called the 'skewer'. The easy way to remember the difference is that in the pin the less valuable piece is in front and, by moving, gives up the more valuable piece behind. In the skewer the more valuable piece is in front and is usually moved out of danger, losing the less valuable piece behind.

*(bottom right)* In this case the Rook is well and truly pinned. It cannot move legally at all, since to do so would expose the King to check. So White would play 1 Bxg2+, Black would reply 1 ... Kxg2, and White would have won the exchange.

Of the two minor pieces, the Bishop has the disadvantage of not being able to jump over pieces or change the colour of the squares to which he can move. But whereas the Knight is brilliant at the double attack (the fork), when it comes to the pin it is the Bishop who excels. Indeed, the Knight cannot pin at all!

Play through the following game, which shows the Bishop at work.

Rosentreter – Hofer (Berlin 1899).

| | | |
|---|---|---|
| 1 | e4 | e5 |
| 2 | Nf3 | Nc6 |
| 3 | Bc4 | Bc5 |
| 4 | 0–0 | Nf6 |
| 5 | d4 | Bxd4 |
| 6 | Nxd4 | Nxd4 |
| 7 | Bg5 | |

(pinning the Knight)

| | | |
|---|---|---|
| 7 | ... | h6 |
| 8 | Bh4 | g5? |

(Black tries to remove the pin, but this is just what White wants)

|   |   |   |
|---|---|---|
| 9 | f4!! | gxf4 |

(or 9 ... gxh4 10 fxe5 Ne6 11 Rxf6, with an excellent attack for White)

| | | |
|---|---|---|
| 10 | Rxf4! | exf4 |
| 11 | Qxd4 | 0–0 |
| 12 | Bxf6 | Qe8 |
| 13 | Bh8! | |

and Black resigns. He cannot prevent mate on g7, since ... f6 is impossible, the pawn being pinned!

This game shows how uncomfortable a defender can feel when a Bishop is tying him down with a pin. A perfect example of the threat being stronger than the execution (until the time comes to finish things off). Such pins play an important part in many openings, as we shall see.

The power of the pin can be really tremendous, as in the following position.

*Diagram 19.2* MacDonnel – Lewis. Black is in a terrible position. He cannot move his King without losing his Rook on e6 which is pinned to the King by the Bishop, and his Rook on e8 is tied (with the

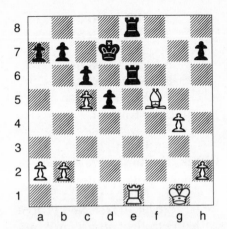

*Diagram 19.2*

King) to the defence of the Rook on e6, which is in fact attacked twice.

The only thing left for Black to do is to try to free things a bit with pawn moves. But this too is hopeless, due to a combination of the pin and the fact that Black cannot escape the pin and still keep in touch with his Rook on e6, because of White's pawn on c5. If the black King could move to d6 he would be all right – that would break the pin and force White to do something about threats like ... Rxe1+. So what if Black had tried 1 ... b6, hoping that White would play 2 cxb6, since this would leave d6 clear for Black's King? White would then have replied 2 b4, so that if Black played 2 ... bxc5 White could recapture and keep the stranglehold on c6.

What is left for Black? He tried 2 ... d4, but this only allowed

White to play 3 Re5!, which made it possible for White's King to cross the e-file to attack Black's Queen's side pawns. Play then continued 3 ... bxc5  4 bxc5 h6  5 Kf2 Re7  6 Ke2, and Black resigned. White would simply have advanced his King's side pawns now, and there would have been nothing Black could do about it. That's the sort of pin to have working for you!

Now consider the following position.

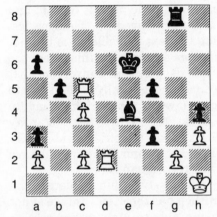

*Diagram 19.3*

*Diagram 19.3* Hansen – Möller (Golz 1976). Remembering what you have learned about pins, how does Black (to play) win from this position?

Now look at this short game.
Kan – Levenfish (Leningrad 1933).

| 1 | e4 | e5 |
| 2 | Nf3 | Nc6 |

| 3 | Bc4 | Nf6 |
| 4 | d4 | exd4 |
| 5 | Ng5 | Ne5 |
| 6 | Bb3 | h6 |
| 7 | f4 | hxg5 |
| 8 | fxe5 | Nxe4 |
| 9 | 0–0 | d5 |
| 10 | exd6 ep | Qxd6 |
| 11 | Bxf7+ | Kd8 |
| 12 | g3 | |

(Black was threatening 12 ... Qxh2 mate)

| 12 | ... | d3! |
| 13 | Qe1 | Qb6+ |
| 14 | Be3 | Bc5 |
| 15 | Rf3 | Bg4 |
| 16 | Bxc5 | Qxc5+ |
| 17 | Re3 | |

(if White had played 17 Qe3 to block the check, Black would have won the Rook on f3 (Bxf3), since White's Queen could not have recaptured, being pinned to the King by Black's Queen. Nor could White have won Black's Queen, since she is protected by the Knight on e4)

| 17 | ... | Be2! |

and White resigned. The only way White could have defended the Rook would have been to play 18 Qc1, but then Black would have rrreplied 18 ... d2!, putting an end to that idea!

Now study the following position, in which Black cleverly uses the Queen pin. Play through the main line first and then the notes.

*Diagram 19.4* Blümich – Alekhine (1941). Black sees that if

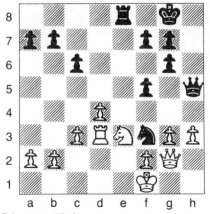

Diagram 19.4

his Queen could reach b5 – pinning the Rook on d3 – he should be able to win. So

| 1 | ... | f4! |
|---|---|---|

(see note (a))

| 2 | gxf4 | Qb5! |
|---|---|---|
| 3 | c4 | |

(see note (b))

| 3 | ... | Qxc4 |
|---|---|---|

(see note (c))

| 4 | Qxf3 | Qxd3+ |
|---|---|---|
| 5 | Kg2 | Qxd4 |

and Black went on to win.

Set up the position after 1 . . . f4! Note (a) – this double attack by the pawn, although unsupported, is killing. Not only does it clear the rank for Black to move his Queen to b5, but it attacks a Knight that cannot move without considerably weakening Black's defences. Look carefully. If the Knight moved anywhere but to c2, Black would play 2 . . . Re1 mate. If the Knight moved to c2 – protecting this mat-ing square – then 2 . . . Nh4! 3 gxh4 Qe2+ (supported by the Rook on e8) and after White's King moved, the black Queen would pick up White's Rook on d3!

Back to the position after 1 . . . f4! If White decided not to take this double-attacking f-pawn, he could play 2 g4, attacking Black's Queen. Then 2 . . . fxe3! 3 gxh5 e2 mate. Remember this mate – it is a very clever one. (Diagram 19.5.)

Reset the position after 1 . . . f4! Suppose White saw this danger and instead of playing 2 g4 fxe3! 3 gxh5, he played 3 Rxe3. Then Black would reply 3 . . . Rxe3!, and if White now took the Queen 4 gxh5, it would be 4 . . . Re1, mate again! If White had taken the Rook 4 fxe3, instead, Black would win after 4 . . . Qb5+.

Try it.

Set up 19.4 again.

Note (b) – after 1 . . . f4! 2 gxf4 Qb5!, instead of playing 3 c4, White could have played 3 Ke2, but then 3 . . . Qxd3+! 4 Kxd3 Ne1+, and Black would have decided the game by forking the King and the Queen. Note (c) – in the actual game Black was able to play 3 . . . Qxc4 because the white Knight was powerless to capture the Queen, since Black would then have had the simple 4 . . . Re1 mate.

That was an exceptionally interesting game, containing as it did a double attack, pins, forks, and several threats. Although the pieces were even to begin with, once Black had played f4 there was nothing White could do to avoid the eventual defeat. Try the various moves from this position for yourself, and you will find that unless Black blunders he will always come out on top, whatever White does.

Now consider the following two positions.

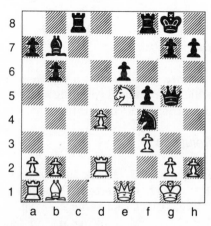

Diagram 19.5

Diagram 19.5 Herberg – Averbach (Stockholm 1954). How does Black (to play) win from this position? Here are three clues: (i) a fork is involved as well as a pin; (ii) White's Rook on d2 dare not move from the second rank because of . . . Qxg2 mate; and (iii) Black's first move is a pin.

Diagram 19.6 Harjet – Ditt (Bremen 1954). How does White (to play) win from this position? A clue

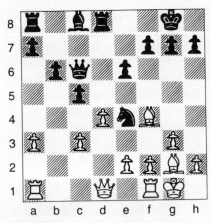

*Diagram 19.6*

— White brings about a position in which his Queen is pinning a pawn, but other pins come into it too!

## Solutions

**Diagram 19.3** Black simply plays 1 ... Rxg2, and after White plays 2 Rxg2, Black replies *not* 2 ... fxg2+ but 2 ... f2!, making use of the fact that the Rook on g2 is pinned. Black's pawn cannot be prevented from promoting.

**Diagram 19.5** Black plays 1 ... Rc1!, because after White is forced to reply 2 Qxc1 (or if 2 Rd1, Black has 2 ... Qxg2 mate), 2 ... Ne2+ (the fork) 3 Rxe2 Qxc1+, and Black has not only gained the Queen for the loss of a Rook and a Knight, but he has many more winning threats. For example, after 4 Kf2, he could play 4 ... Qd1 threatening White's

d-pawn, or 4 ... Ba6, attacking the Rook, and it looks as though White would never disentangle his Queen's side pieces. Try these moves for yourself.

**Diagram 19.6** This is an unusually clever use of the pin. After White plays 1 d5!, Black must capture this pawn or his Knight on e4 falls at once. We have three clearcut variations: (a) 1 ... Rxd5 2 Bxe4 Rxd1 3 Bxc6, and White has gained a Queen and a Knight for the loss of a Queen and a pawn. Reset 19.7. After 1 d5! (b) 1 ... exd5 2 Bxe4, and the d-pawn is pinned (2 ... dxe4?? allows 3 Qxd8+ and mate next move); or (set up 19.7 again) 1 d5! (c) 1 ... Qxd5 2 Bxe4!, and this time the black Queen is pinned! As 2 ... Qxe4?? would allow 3 Qxd8 mate, Black loses the exchanges after 2 ... Qxd1 3 Raxd1 Rxd1 4 Rxd1 Bb7 (or the Rook is lost) 5 Bxb7, etc.

Note that in the diagram position White's pin of the Knight by his Bishop cannot be exploited, since 1 Qc2? putting a second attacker onto the Knight, would allow 1 ... Bb7, adding a second defender.

# Unit 20

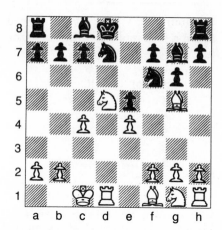

*Diagram 20.1*

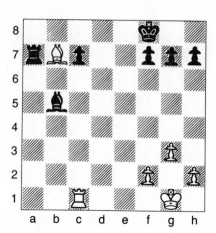

*Diagram 20.2*

## More Pins

A Rook pin can be particularly effective early in a game, when a file is opened quickly. Here is a good example of this.

|   |       |       |
|---|-------|-------|
| 1 | d4    | Nf6   |
| 2 | c4    | g6    |
| 3 | Nc3   | Bg7   |
| 4 | e4    | d6    |
| 5 | Bg5   | e5?   |

(Black really should have castled)

|   |       |       |
|---|-------|-------|
| 6 | dxe5  | dxe5  |
| 7 | Qxd8+ | Kxd8  |

(Black had no alternative here, but his Knight on f6 is now in a really nasty pin)

|   |       |       |
|---|-------|-------|
| 8 | Nd5   | Nbd7  |
| 9 | 0–0–0!|       |

and now (diag. 20.1), after only 9 moves, Black is helpless and must lose a piece.

White threatens Nxf6, and Black's other Knight (on d7) could not recapture, since it is pinned by the Rook on d1. If Black played 10 . . . Bxf6, White would simply recapture, with his own Bishop from g5 with a check and when the black King moved the Rook on h8 would be lost. Black cannot break the pin by playing 9 . . . Ke8, since

this would allow Nxc7+, winning the other Rook for White on the next move.

In the next example the power of the pin is even more striking, if not incredible. Set up the position on your board to see the full elegance of Black's play.

*Diagram 20.2* Lewis – Pines (Cape Town 1955). White to move. Black was threatening to capture White's Bishop on b7, so White played 1 Rxc7, thinking that he would easily be able to escape from the resulting pin of his Bishop by playing Rc8+ on the next move. But that only promised to work because Black would have to get out of check immediately, leaving the white Bishop able to move away from the Rook's attack. So Black of course removed the possibility of the check by playing 1 . . . Be8! White then decided to bring his King into play

and played 2 Kf1, but Black had another excellent idea. He played 2 . . . g6!, and play continued 3 Ke1 Kg7, which meant that Black had removed any possibility of a check from White's Rook on c8. Now Black was actually threatening to win the exchange, giving up his Bishop for White's Rook, by playing the Bishop to b5 and then to a6. White thought he could counter this threat by playing 4 Rc8, attacking Black's Bishop while offering his own in fair exchange. But then 4 . . . Bd7 5 Rb8 Ra1+ 6 Kd2 Rb1! and White's Bishop is pinned the other way and now White could not avoid the forced loss of the exchange after 7 . . . Bc6. Beautiful, isn't it?

Here is a similar example from a world championship match.

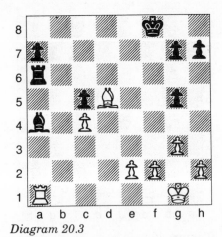

Diagram 20.3

Diagram 20.3 Euwe – Alekhine (1935). White is pinning Black's Bishop, but on his next move Black could remove this pin by playing 1 ... Bb5!, since if White replied 2 cxb5, Black would play 2 ... Rxa1+ and win the exchange. What can White do to stop this? He could try playing 1 Ra3, threatening 2 Rf3+ and getting his Rook off the a-file so that Black could not capture him. But 1 ... g4 would stop this, since the Rook could not then give check on f3.

White in fact found a brilliant move that meant that if Black *did* play 1 ... Bb5, White would actually win the Bishop. See if you can spot that move. (If you do, you can feel delighted with your progress to date.)

Now look at the following game. It contains a terrible mistake, which Alekhine relates was made by four amateurs who played against him in a consultation game in Majorca, in 1935.

| 1 | e4 | c6 |
| 2 | d4 | d5 |
| 3 | Nc3 | dxe4 |
| 4 | Nxe4 | Nf6 |
| 5 | Bd3 | Qxd4 |
| 6 | Nf3 | Qd8 |
| 7 | Qe2 | Nbd7?? |

How can four people, playing together, agree on a move like this? Can you see how fatal a move it is? White's next move is given at the end of this Unit, but let us hope that you spot it before you need to look. You will find it hard to understand how four players missed White's next move, but it is true to say that many players fail to see when a pawn is pinned. After all, a 'humble' pawn is easily forgotten.

Let us examine some more examples of the pinned pawn,

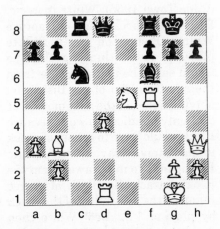

Diagram 20.4

beginning with a particular favourite of ours.

Diagram 20.4 Coggan – Foster (Boston 1937). It is White to move. In this quiet-looking position Black must have been 'knocked for six' when White produced 1 Qxh7+!! Kxh7 2 Rh5+ Kg8 3 Ng6!, which threatened checkmate by 4 Rh8. Black was powerless to stop it – he could not capture the Knight with his f-pawn, since the pawn was *pinned* by White's Bishop on b3!

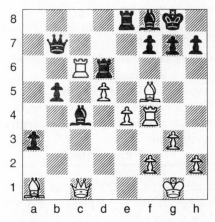

Diagram 20.5

Diagram 20.5 Sacharov – Cherepkov (Alma-Ata 1969). 1 Bxh7+! Kxh7 2 Rxd6 (see note (a)) Bxd6 3 Rh4+ Kg8 (if 3 ... Kg6, 4 Rg4+ mates in two moves) 4 Rh8+! Kxh8 5 Qh6+! Kg8 6 Qxg7 mate.

Note (a) – By capturing this Rook,

White removed one guard from h6 and, as Black had to recapture with the Bishop from f8, the move also removed the guard on Black's pawn on g7.

Such sequences of moves may not seem so obvious until they are shown to you, but by constant practice and use of pins, forks, double attacks, threats, etc., there will come a time when you are able to spot them in your own games.

Here is a chance of a bit more practice on your own.

*Diagram 20.6* Smyslov – Fuller (Hastings 1968–69). White to move and win.

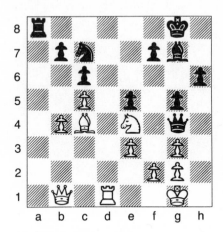

*Diagram 20.6*

*Diagram 20.7* Mädler – Uhlmann (Aschersleben 1963). Black to move and win.

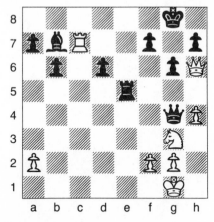

*Diagram 20.7*

*Diagram 20.8* Abrahams – Thynne (Liverpool 1930). White to move and win. A clue – If you have any difficulty with this, look back to Coggan – Foster (Fig. 118).

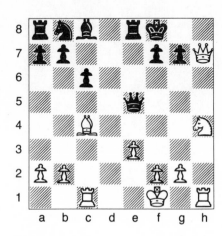

*Diagram 20.8*

## Solutions

**Diagram 20.3** Did you see that 1 Ra2! prevents 1 ... Bb5, since this would still be answered by 2 cxb5 but White's Rook is now protected by the Bishop? A great idea that allowed White to keep the black pieces tied down and eventually won the game for him. (Euwe went on to win the world championship!)

**Diagram 20.6** If you saw 1 Nf6+! Bxf6 2 Qg6+!, you did well, but White now had to make sure that he had a win. (Don't forget that his Rook on d1 is now unguarded!) After 2 ... Bg7 3 Qxf7+ Kh8, White had 4 Rd7!, winning at once because 4 ... Rg8 would allow 5 Qxg8 mate, and otherwise White had 5 Qxg7 mate.

**Diagram 20.7** You either see this or you don't, but all the pointers are there for you. Black wins by 1 ... Re1+ 2 Kh2 (or 2 Nf1 Qxg2 mate) 2 ... Rh1+! – this was the difficult move to see, but remember that this Unit is about pins – 3 Kxh1 (or Nxh1 Qxg2 mate) 3 ... Qh3+ 4 Kg1 Qxg2 mate.

**Diagram 20.8** You probably found the main line of attack 1 Qg8+! Kxg8 2 Ng6!, using the fact that the 'f' pawn is pinned, when Black cannot prevent Rh8 mate. However, did you consider what you would do if Black had tried to escape by 1 . . . Ke7 2 Qxf7+ Kd8 ? Don't worry if you didn't. After all, you have a sound position with plenty of good moves, so you can now sit back, perhaps as White did, and work out the best way of finishing Black off. White played 3 Ng6! and play continued Qxb2? 4 Rd1+ Bd7 5 Qxe8+! Kxe8 6 Rh8 mate. A very fine finish.

But what if Black had kept his Rook protected by playing 3 . . . Qe4 ? (From the position in diagram 20.8, 1 Qg8+! Ke7 2 Qxf7+ Kd8 3 Ng6 Qe4). Could White have driven the Queen away? Of course, 4 Rd1+ Bd7 5 Rh4! would have forced the black Queen to give up her protection of the Rook, and then 5 . . . Qc2 6 Qxe8+! Kxe8 7 Rh8 mate, as before. Did you see some of these possibilities? Good for you if you saw more than half of them.

Incidentally, did you spot Alekhine's eighth move as White in the game against four amateurs? After the amateurs' terrible blunder, 7 . . . Nbd7??, Alekhine had 8 Nd6 mate!

# Unit 21

## When is a Pin Not a Pin?

An unusual but extremely effective type of pin is the 'double' or 'cross-pin'. This is shown in the following examples.

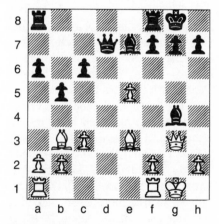

*Diagram 21.1*

*Diagram 21.1* Dahl – Schulz (Berlin 1956). Who would think that in three moves from this seemingly evenly balanced position, White could win a piece? Set up the position on your board and watch closely. 1 e6! Bxe6 2 Bd4 (threatening mate by Qxg7) 2 ... f6. Black could not play 2 ... Bf6 because White would reply 3 Bxf6 and the g-pawn would be unable to recapture, since it is pinned. What about 2 ... g6? Well, White would then play 3 Qe5, with a mating threat along the diagonal. So, for Black, 2 ... f6 seems to be the best move. But no! White could then employ the cross-pin, by playing 3 Qg4! Black's Bishop on e6 is now pinned two ways and must be lost, since if Black played 3 ... Kf7, White would reply 4 Rfe1, and 3 ... f5? would allow the immediate 4 Qxg7 mate.

Although the explanation of these 'ifs', 'buts' and 'maybe's' often seem complicated, we hope that you are beginning to see some of the possibilities even before they are explained to you.

*Diagram 21.2* Gendel – Sushkevitz (USSR 1956). Black to move.

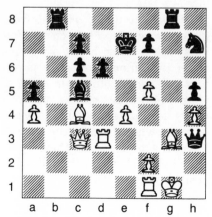

*Diagram 21.2*

The first thing to note is that White's pawn on f2 is pinned, so that after Black plays 1 ... Rxg3+!, White has to play 2 Rxg3. Black then plays Rg8! and the white Rook on g3 is pinned two ways – to the King along the g-file and to the Queen along the third rank. So, White is forced to reply 3 Rxg8, allowing Black to win White's Queen, with a net profit on the transaction to Black.

The previous exercise should help you to solve the next one.

*Diagram 21.3* White to move. It looks all over for White, whose Queen is pinned by the black Rook. Can you see a way out?

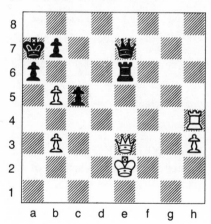

*Diagram 21.3*

And now the explanation of the title of this Unit – 'When is a pin not a pin?' Look at the following two opening traps.

| | | |
|---|---|---|
| 1 | e4 | e5 |
| 2 | Nf3 | Nc6 |
| 3 | d4 | exd4 |
| 4 | Bc4 | d6 |
| 5 | c3 | dxc3 |
| 6 | Nxc3 | Bg4 |
| 7 | 0–0. | |

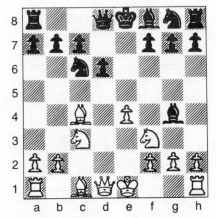

*Diagram 21.4*

*Diagram 21.4* Now Black has pinned White's Knight on f3, but he dare not take advantage of this right away by playing 7 . . . Ne5?, because this would lead to 8 Nxe5! Bxd1 9 Bxf7+ Ke7 10 Nd5 mate. Another poor move for Black would be 7 . . . Nge7?, since 8 Bxf7+! Kxf7 9 Ng5+, followed by 10 Qxg4, would win back the pawn for White and leave Black with a weakened position.

You may wonder why White did not play 7 Bxf7+ instead of castling, but we'll leave this as an additional exercise for you. The answer is at the end of this Unit.

Here is the second opening trap.

| | | |
|---|---|---|
| 1 | d4 | d5 |
| 2 | c4 | e6 |
| 3 | Nc3 | Nf6 |
| 4 | Bg5. | |

Now White has pinned Black's Knight on f6 – or has he?

One often played reply for Black is 4 . . . Nbd7, which allows 5 cxd5 exd5 6 Nxd5?, apparently winning a pawn for White because of the 'pin' on Black's Knight on f6. But Black replies 6 . . . Nxd5!!, and if White takes the black Queen 7 Bxd8, Bb4+ forces White to interpose his Queen on d2. So 8 Qd2 Bxd2+ 9 Kxd2 Kxd8, and Black has gained a Knight for the loss of a pawn.

The lesson to be learned from these two examples is clear. You must always watch out for times when the pinned piece *can* move. Some players make the mistake of simply pinning pieces without really thinking about what they are doing, or whether or not the pin will have any effect upon their opponent's play. Consider the following position, for example.

*Diagram 21.5* von Popiel – Marco (Monte Carlo 1902). White had pinned Black's Bishop on d4 and was now ready to capture it. Black, to

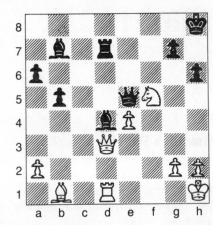

*Diagram 21.5*

move, could see no way of saving this piece and resigned. It is often difficult to believe anything in chess – even if it seems obvious. What both players had missed was that the 'pinned' Bishop could have moved away: he could have moved to g1 and threatened . . . Qxh2 mate! To avoid this sudden defeat, White would have had to capture the Bishop, and then his Queen would have been lost. Try moving the white Queen to h3 to stop the mate – and see what happens.

If master chess players can miss such a move, you can excuse yourself for missing things from time to time. The attraction of chess lies in the fact that there is always the challenge of trying to find the best moves, in the right order, at the right time, etc. Sometimes you will hit upon moves so brilliant as to be dazzling, as White did in the following position.

*Diagram 21.6* Onescius – Gama (Switzerland 1956). Black is threatening ... Qxh2+, followed by ... Qh1 mate or ... Qg2 mate.

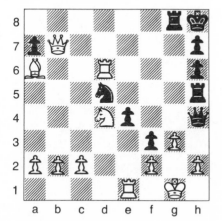

*Diagram 21.6*

What, if anything, can White do about it? Well, let us not give up hope until we have tried all the possibilities.

The most obvious thing to ask ourselves is can we capture the black Queen? After all, she is en prise to the g-pawn. No, the g-pawn is pinned. Can we then, do anything to break this pin? It has to be something that would work at once because Black's mating threat is an immediate one. (If you are able to solve this problem, you can be sure of winning a few chess trophies in the future!)

Do try to find the moves before reading on.

White found a quite brilliant solution. First of all he cleared the e-file for his Rook (on e1) by playing 1 Nxf3!, attacking the black Queen but more important controlling the vital h2 square. Black recaptured the Knight by playing 1 ... exf3. Then White played 2 Qg7+!!, Black replied 2 ... Kxg7 and White was able to capture the black Queen by playing 3 gxh4, since the g-pawn was no longer pinned! If Black had captured the Queen with his Rook, 2 ... Rxg7, then 3 Re8+ (made possible by White's first move) 3 ... Rg8 4 Rxg8+ Kxg8, and once again the pin would be gone, so White could play 5 gxh4 quite legally.

The game eventually ended in a draw, but when you bear in mind the problem White seemed to have in the position shown in diag. 21.6, it was a remarkable escape for him.

Now it's your turn to find the best moves.

*Diagram 21.7* Olsen – Jacobsen (Aarhus 1953). White's Queen is attacked, so White decided to pin the attacking Bishop by playing 1 Rexd5, since if Black played 1 ... Bxc6, 2 Rxd8 would be checkmate. But before Black plays ... Bxc6, there is another move he can make in reply to 1 Rexd5, that would put an end to White's plan. A clue – the pinner becomes the pinned.

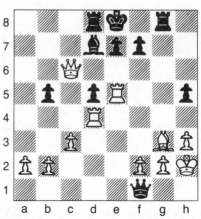

*Diagram 21.7*

*Diagram 21.8* Soos – Teschner (West Germany 1970). Black played 1 ... Qd5, threatening ... Qh1 mate. If White replied 2 Rxf4, then 2 ... Qh1+ 3 Kf2 Qh2+ 4 Kf1 Rxf4+ 5 Nf2 Qxg3, and Black would win easily. If White replied 2 Bc4, pinning the black Queen, would he do any better?

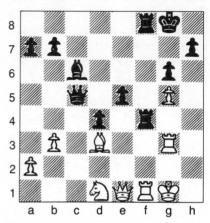

*Diagram 21.8*

## Solutions

Diagram 21.3 White sets up a cross-pin after playing 1 b6+!, to which Black is forced to reply ... Kxb6 (or be mated on the back rank). White plays 2 Rh6!, and Black will lose his Rook on the next move, or, after 2 ... Rxh6 3 Qxe7, his Queen.

Diagram 21.4 It is easy to imagine that White played 7 Bxf7+ and forced Black to reply 7 ... Kxf7, when 8 Ng5+ would win the Bishop on g4 for White. (The black King would move out of check, and White would play 9 Qxg4.) However, Black would *not* have to move his King out of check! He could play 8 ... Qxg5! Then if White played 9 Bxg5, Black would reply 9 ... Bxd1, and then after 10 Rxd1 Black would have gained a Knight for the loss of a pawn. So White would have to try 9 ... Qb3+. But Black has another brilliant move in reserve, 9 ... Be6! Play would then continue 10 Qxb7 Qxg2! 11 Rf1 Bh3! 12 Qxa8 Qxf1+, with an easy win for Black.

Diagram 21.7 Black played 1 ... Qxg2+! and White resigned, since not only would Black have exchanged Queens after 2 Kxg2 Bxc6, he would also capture the pinned white Rook. What a blow to White, who appeared to be so favourably placed in the diagram position.

Diagram 21.8 If White replied 2 Bc4, then 2 ... Rxf1+ 3 Qxf1 Rxf1+ 4 Kxf1 Bb5!, and White's dangerous looking Bishop would itself be pinned!

# Unit 22

## More about Rook Endings

As was mentioned earlier, the Rook is a piece that excels in the end game, where it has lots of space in which to operate. Then, one of its main tasks is to stop the enemy pawns from promoting.

Consider the following position, for example: diagram 22.1.

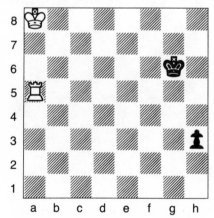

Diagram 22.1

Black's pawn needs only two moves to promote. Can White, to move, stop him?

Well, if the White Rook is to capture the pawn without being captured in return (giving Black a draw) it has to reach the pawn before the black King can come to the support of the little fellow.

White plays 1 Ra3! At first glance you may be rather surprised by this move. After all it encourages the pawn to take a step nearer to the Queening square. But when Black replies 1 . . . h2, White immediately gets the Rook behind the unprotected pawn by playing 2 Rh3. Now, all is clear, and the pawn is lost.

White obviously had to get the Rook behind or in front of the pawn. He could not play 1 Rh5 from the diagram position since the black King would have captured him immediately. Nor could the Rook get in front of the pawn – there simply wasn't time.

If White had played 1 Ra1, Black would have replied 1 . . . Kg5, and when White continued 2 Rh1, Black could have defended the pawn by playing 2 . . . Kg4, and the King would then have stayed with the pawn and have shepherded it to promotion, winning the Rook for it.

The sequence of moves actually played from the diagram position – 1 Ra3! h2 2 Rh3 h1=Q+ 3 Rxh1 – can be called a 'manoeuvre', since the moves were aimed at a particular objective, namely the quickest and safest capture of the dangerous black pawn.

By playing 1 Ra3, White actually *forced* Black to move the pawn on, otherwise it would have fallen next move to 2 Rxh3. But by playing 1 . . . h2, Black did the forcing, for if White had not then played 2 Rh3, the pawn could have promoted next move. (Of course, having forced the pawn one more move away from King, White could have played 2 Ra1, and then 3 Rh1, but why take a longer way round?)

White won Black's pawn by what could be called an 'end-game combination'. Always look for combinations. Look for, and examine, *forced* sequences of moves since they will teach you a lot about the position – even if you decide, having examined them, not to actually play them. You will be learning about threats, defences and manoeuvres. You will be practising end-game calculation, learning to be accurate, analysing, and developing your strength as a player.

Now look back to diagram 22.1 and ask yourself what would have happened if it had been Black to move?

White would still win the pawn because the black King could not cross the 'barbed wire fence' that White's Rook has, in effect, strung across the fifth rank. So if Black, to move first, played 1 . . . h2, then by 2 Ra1! Kg5 3 Rh1 Kg4 4 Rxh2, White would capture the pawn just one move before the black King could support it. This shows how precise your calculations have to be!

Although we have shown you the best (quickest) ways for White to win the black pawn, he could have tried bringing his King across to help. But he would have to be very careful, as we shall see.

Set up diagram 22.1 on your board again and let us try a few moves with the white King.

1 Kb7 Kh6 2 Kc6 Kg6

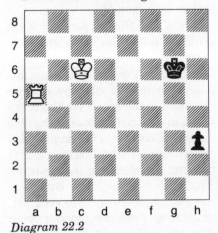

Diagram 22.2

What would be wrong with 3 Kd5? You will find the answer at the end of this Unit but do try to answer the question before you look.

White would actually play 3 Re5, and after 3 . . . Kh6 4 Kd5 Kg6. See diagram 22.3.

White's obvious move would seem to be 5 Ke4, bringing his King nearer the pawn. But this would be a dreadful blunder. Why? Again try to find out before looking up the answer at the end of the Unit.

White would actually play 5 Kd4, and then play would continue 5 . . . Kh6 6 Re8 Kg5 7 Ke3 and White would win without any trouble.

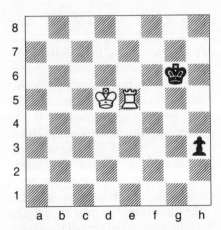

Diagram 22.3

Exciting wasn't it? There were traps to be avoided and White had to play very carefully in this line. How much easier it was to play the simple winning line 1 Ra3 from diagram 22.1 in the first place. But it was worthwhile showing you the longer variation using the white King as you will sometimes find yourself with a similar position where you will *have* to bring your King across the board. When this occurs just remember to watch out for traps such as those shown here.

Now consider the following position, which is slightly different from the one shown in diagram 22.1.

What difference, if any, does it make whether it is (a) White to move or (b) Black to move? Answers at the end of this Unit.

Now turn your full attention to the following position.

We are going to spend some time

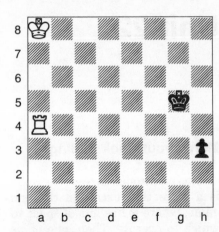

Diagram 22.4

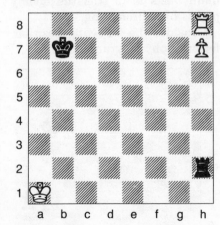

Diagram 22.5

on this position so consider carefully the strengths and weaknesses in each side's situation. Look at the position first from Black's point of view. What would you play as Black here?

The black Rook is doing two important jobs at the moment. On the one hand he has set up the familiar 'barbed wire fence' across the second rank, preventing White's King from getting into the action. He is also tying down White's Rook to the defence of the lone h-pawn. So you would probably (wisely) choose to leave the Rook where it is and move the King. But move the King where? Only one of the following possibilities is correct: 1 ... Kc7, 1 ... Ka7, or 1 ... Kb6. Which move is correct and what is wrong with the other two? You will find the answers at the end of this Unit but do work on them yourself before looking and be absolutely certain you understand all this before you move on.

Now, back to diagram 22.5. This time consider the position with White to move first. As White cannot move his Rook immediately without losing the pawn, he is forced to bring his King across to g1 to force Black's Rook away from h2 where it is doing the two important jobs mentioned earlier. There is no need to write out the moves because all Black can do is wait, by moving his King between b7 and a7, until the position in diagram 22.6 is reached.

Now the black Rook is attacked and he must stay on the h-file. Why? Well, there are two simple ways that White could win if Black played 1 ... Ra2, for example. What are these two easy wins? See if you can work them out for yourself before looking at the answers at the end of this Unit.

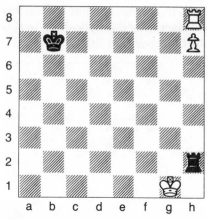

*Diagram 22.6*

Having found the dangers in Black moving his Rook from the h-file you will appreciate why the best White can do is to get to the position shown in diagram 22.7.

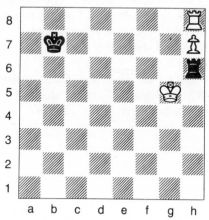

*Diagram 22.7*

Black to play.

Now we can see what White has been after. He needed to get his King close enough to the pawn to protect it, move his Rook from the promotion square and then Queen his pawn. This leaves Black with the choice of either exchanging his Rook for the new Queen – and playing on, a Rook down, until he is (or should be) checkmated – or playing his Rook against White's Queen and Rook with the same result.

As the black Rook had the barbed wire fence across the second rank, White had to get his King to the pawn by a roundabout route along the first rank and then up the g-file, banking on the fact that Black *had* to keep his Rook on the h-file or allow the pawn to promote even earlier.

So what can Black play from Diagram 22.7? Well, 1 ... Rh1 is as good as anything here. White would reply 2 Kg6, and be threatening to move his Rook away so Black would be forced to give check by playing 2 ... Rg1+, and play would continue 3 Kh6 Rh1+. But this would be good enough for Black. The only way White could escape the checks would be to work his way back down the board with his King to attack the worrying Rook. Then, however, the Rook would simply take command of the h-file again and White would be back where he started. Neither side could make any real progress and there would be nothing more to be done than to shake hands and agree a draw.

But once again it was exciting. If you look deeply into each move you make, each position you reach, each decision you have to take, you will find that the whole game of chess is full of excitement. This way you will get a great deal of enjoyment and satisfaction out of your play – win, lose or draw.

Still on the theme of a Rook's pawn on the seventh rank look at the following position:

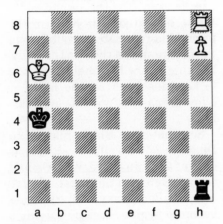

Diagram 22.8

After White plays 1 Kb6, Black must reply 1 ... Kb4 (to stop 2 Ra8+, followed by the black King moving out of check and the white pawn promoting next move, protected by the Rook on a8) Play would then go on 2 Kc6 Kc4 3 Kd6 Kd4, and the crafty black King would continue to shelter from the checks by using White's King as a shield. So how could White put a stop to this and win the game? Look for a 'combination', and then check your solution at the end of this Unit.

We now come to what is probably the most interesting position in this Unit – a position full of surprises.

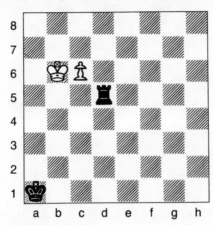

Diagram 22.9

White plays 1 c7, threatening promotion of the pawn and giving Black the problem of how to stop it. Could Black draw if he played 1 ... Rd2, and then after 2 c8=Q+, 2 ... Rb2+?

Back to diagram 22.9. After White plays 1 c7, Black decides to check by playing 1 ... Rd6+.

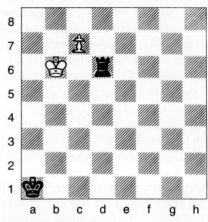

Diagram 22.10

Now the white King is in check and must move out of check immediately. But he would be wrong to move to b7, a5 or c5. Why? Which is the worst of these moves?

Back to diagram 22.10. Play continues 2 Kb5 Rd5+ 3 Kb4 Rd4+ 4 Kb3 Rd3+ 5 Kc2, and it looks all over for Black.

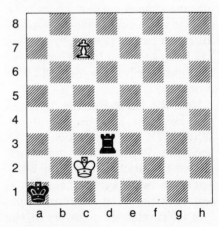

Diagram 22.11

Black cannot get at the pawn, and if he doesn't move the Rook immediately he will lose it. What a predicament!

But Black comes up with a clever idea. Look at 5 . . . Rd4!

(a) Why does Black play this move?
(b) Could White do anything about the threat?
(c) Could White go on to win – or would the game be drawn?

Think carefully about these questions and do try hard to answer them *before* looking up the solutions at the end of the Unit. Above all, don't give up too easily. Try out all the possible defences for Black against the threat of White's pawn promoting.

You certainly have had a lot to think about in this Unit but, before moving on, consider this one final position.

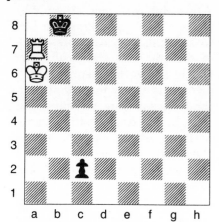

*Diagram 22.12*

This time it is Black who is

threatening to promote a pawn. Fortunately for White it is his turn to move, but what can he do about the promotion threat? If you have studied this Unit properly there is a good chance that you will find the solution without needing to look it up.

*Solutions*

Diagram 22.2   Instead of thinking of the White Rook's control of the fifth rank as a barbed wire fence, think of it as an electronic barrier. Just look at what would happen if White *does* play 3 Kd5? This move would 'short-circuit' the barrier allowing the black King to cross without danger, since the white King would be blocking the Rook's control. Indeed, after 3 . . . Kf5! 4 Kd4+ Kg4! (stopping 5 Rh5) 5 Ke5 h2 6 Ra1 Kg3 7 Ke2 Kg2, Black would promote his pawn and force a draw. You see how easy it can be to spoil everything with just one careless move?

Diagram 22.3   5 Ke4? would be not only careless, it would be 'criminal', for after Black replied 5 . . . h2!, it is *he* who would win! White could try 6 Re6+, hoping for 6 . . . Kf7?, when 7 Rh6 would stop the pawn, but after 6 . . . Kg5! instead, 7 Re5+ Kg4!, and White has run out of checks. He might have had a chance now with 8 Re8, threatening to check on g8 and h8, except for the

fact that the black pawn Queens *with check*, and Black would be expected to win the ending with King and Queen against King and Rook.

Diagram 22.4   You probably spotted that White could not win from this position even with first move. Black's King being one square nearer the pawn than in diagram 22.1 makes all the difference. After 1 Ra3, Black would not this time be forced to advance the pawn but he could defend it by playing 1 . . . Kg4 or 1 . . . Kh4. If it were black to move from diagram 22.4, he would then have the threat of advancing his pawn, because after 1 . . . h2! 2 Ra1, the King can reach his pawn in time by 2 . . . Kg4 3 Kb7 Kg3 4 Kc6 Kg2 5 Ra2+ Kg1 (or . . . Kg3 or . . . Kh3) and White cannot drive the King away from the pawn, so the result would be a draw.

Diagram 22.5   1 . . . Ka7! is correct. It should be fairly easy to see that 1 . . . Kb6? would enable White to play 2 Rb8+, followed by the promotion of his pawn, since the Queening square would now be free. Whatever Black replied, even threatening the white Rook by 2 . . . Ka7, or 2 . . . Kc7, White's promotion by 3 h8=Q, would protect his Rook and attack the enemy Rook, forcing Black to play 3 . . . Rxh8. Then, after White had recaptured by playing 4 Rxh8, he would be left with a King and a Rook against the lone black King, and would go on to win.

The other possibility, 1 . . . Kc7?, leads to a very nasty trap. White would reply 2 Ra8!, and if Black captured the pawn (2 . . . Rxh7) White would play 3 Ra7+, and be able to pick up the black Rook across the board when the King moves out of check.

Remember this idea since it can come up quite often in this type of ending.

Diagram 22.6  You probably saw one and perhaps both of the ways that White could win after Black played 1 . . . Ra2.
(a) 1 . . . Ra2 2 Rb8+! Kxb8 3 h8=Q+, and it won't be long before the Queen picks up the Rook by a *double attack*. Try this out with an opponent and see how long Black can last before losing the Rook, and then the game.
(b) 1 . . . Ra2 2 Rg8 (or Rf8, Re8 or Rd8) followed by the promotion of the pawn. Simple, but just as effective as (a). You may even prefer this way.

Diagram 22.8  After 1 Kb6 Kb4 2 Kc6 Kc4 3 Kd6 Kd4, White would continue across the board towards the pawn with 4 Ke6 Ke4 5 Kf6 Kf4 (Black still craftily used White's King as a shield but now it is White's turn to produce a good idea). 6 Rf8!!, forcing 6 . . . Rxh7,

when 7 Kg6+ would win the Rook.

Diagram 22.9  Black could not draw after 1 c7 Rd2 2 c8=Q Rb2+, since if play continued 3 Ka5 Ra2+ 4 Kb4 Rb2+ 5 Kc3, White should win with a Queen against a Rook (not an easy win, though).

Of course, White must not move his King to the c-file too early, since this would allow Black to play . . . Rc2+, either winning the Queen or exchanging it for the Rook. For example, 5 Kc4?? Rc2+, and after the King has moved out of the check, 6 . . . Rxc8.

Note that Black could have drawn by playing 1 . . . Rd2 if his King had originally been on b1 instead of a1, since after 2 c8=Q Rb2+ 3 Ka5 Ra2+ 4 Kb4 Rb2+ 5 Kc3? Black would then have 5 . . . Rc2+(!), winning.

Diagram 22.10  Let us deal with the worst move first. If White played 1 Ka5??, Black would even *win* after playing 1 . . . Rc6, picking up the pawn.

The other two King moves are bad only because they they would allow Black to get away with a draw.

After 1 Kb7?, 1 . . . Rd7! *pins* the pawn and would allow Black to exchange it on the next move for the Rook, and after 1 Kc5?, 1 . . . Rd1!, followed by 2 Rc1+, etc., would enable Black to draw, again by exchanging Rook for pawn.

Diagram 22.11  This provides the longest, most difficult and probably the most enjoyable exercise set for you in this Unit. Don't worry if you didn't see everything, but give yourself a pat on the back if you did!
(a) The idea behind 5 . . . Rd4!, is to bring about a draw by forcing *stalemate*. After White plays 6 c8=Q?, Black would reply 6 . . . Rc4+!, and force 7 Qxc4.
(b) Yes, White could do something about the threat. He could promote to a Rook rather than a Queen!
(c) But, even with a Rook, could White win? Let us think about it carefully. After playing 6 c8=R!, White is threatening mate on a8, so 6 . . . Ka2 would not help Black. As the black Rook has no useful checks he has only one way to stop the mate. He must play 6 . . . Ra4!. Many players would now give up for White, but not you! After White plays 3 Kb3!, attacking the Rook, we suddenly have a complete switch of direction by the White Rook which is now threatening mate on c1! This is a very important part of the Rook's powers, so remember it well. In the final position there is nothing Black can do to stop checkmate. He can only postpone it for a while by giving up his Rook (7 . . . Rb4+)

Now, go back to diagram 22.9 and play through the whole line again. What a beautiful sequence of moves it is.

1 c7 Rd6+ 2 Kb5 Rd5+ 3 Kb4 Rd4+

4 Kb3 Rd3+ 5 Kc2 Rd4! 6 c8=R!
Ra4! 7 Kb3 Rb4+ 8 Kxb4, etc.

Diagram 22.12. Well, did the
important clue come to your mind
as you studied this position? If it
did, give yourself another pat on the
back. If it didn't, you should look a
little more deeply into things in the
future.

White saves this particular game
by using the stalemate idea once
again. He plays 1 Rb7+ Kc8 (not 1
... Ka8??, Since 2 Rc7 would win
comfortably tor White) 2 Rb5!!
c1=Q 3 Rc5+! Qxc5, stalemate.
And this time, promoting to a Rook
wouldn't help!

# Unit 23

## Overworked Pieces

We have seen how loose pieces can be captured by means of a double attack. We have also won material by using the pin. In such cases, we could say that the defender made a mistake, either by leaving his men unprotected or by allowing an unpleasant pin. The defender can also make another very common mistake which is not so obvious at first sight. He can easily forget that one or more of his pieces have been given too much work to do. They are, in fact, overstretched, overloaded, overworked. Whichever word you choose the result is the same, and a piece that has too much to do can be exploited − in other words, advantage can be taken of the overloading.

Diagram 23.1 shows what we mean using a simple example from master chess.

*Diagram 23.1* Fuster − Sämisch (Trencanske Teplice 1941). Black's Knight on e8 is guarding the Queen and the g-pawn. But he cannot properly do both in this particular position, as we shall see. After 1

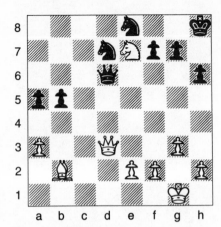

*Diagram 23.1*

Bxg7+ Black is in trouble. If he replies 1 . . . Nxg7 he leaves his Queen unguarded and White immediately takes it with 2 Qxd6, and wins. If Black replies to 1 Bxg7+ with Kxg7, White still wins the black Queen by playing 2 Nf5+ − a fork!

In other words, Black's Knight was overworked. He could not cope with both jobs at once, and White found a way of taking advantage of the fact.

Now look at the next position.

*Diagram 23.2* Najdorf − Amateur (Simultaneous 1942). The first thing to note is that the black Queen is stopping White from playing Nd7 mate. She is tied down to the defence of the d7 square. Let us see how grandmaster Najdorf exploits this weakness in the following play. He first goes 1 Qh5, threatening mate on f7 and forcing

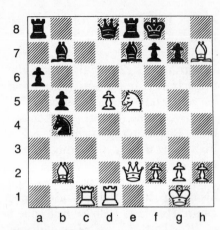

*Diagram 23.2*

the reply 1 . . . Bxd5 so the Bishop can protect (for a moment, at least) f7. (If 1 Qh5 g6 2 Qh6 mates.)

Now comes 2 Rxd5! Qxd5 and we can see what Najdorf has in mind. Black's Queen has been forced into the position of having to defend both d7 *and* f7. Even a Queen cannot serve two masters, so 3 Qxf7+ Qxf7 4 Nd7 mate.

White's third move dragged the black Queen away from the defence of d7. This 'deflection' (as chess problemists call it) is all part and parcel of the way we can exploit an overworked piece. Here's another example:

*Diagram 23.3* Nimzovitch − Marshall (New York 1927). Black's Knight is pinned two ways, but is guarded twice by the Queen and the King. If the black Queen could be deflected White could win the Knight − and go on to checkmate

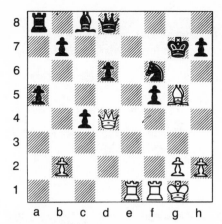

*Diagram 23.3*

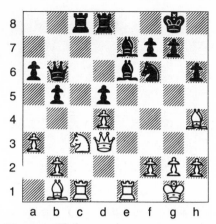

*Diagram 23.4*

Black. How does Nimzovitch achieve this deflection? 1 Re8!, taking advantage of the fact that Queen cannot guard f6 and e8 at the same time. Now, after 1 . . . Qxe8 2 Qxf6+ Kg8 3 Bh6! (threatening Qg7 mate) Black is lost, since 3 . . . Qd7 fails to 4 Qf8 mate, and 3 . . . Qf7 allows 4 Qd8+ Qf8 5 Qxf8 mate. Here is a more complicated position which is well worth spending some time on.

*Diagram 23.4* Szily – Bobotsov. Let us look at some of the Black pieces and the work they are doing.

(1) Black's Knight on f6 is stopping Qh7+. In fact, if Black had a Rook on f8, 1 Bxf6 Bxf6 2 Qh7+ would be mate. (A Knight on f8 would, of course, protect h7.)

(2) Black's Bishop on e6 is not only guarding the d-pawn and a Rook, he is stopping a mating attack. How? Well, suppose that the

Bishop were on d7 instead of e6. This allows 1 Bxf6 Bxf6 2 Qh7+ Kf8 3 Qh8 mate – because White's Rook on e1 would prevent the King from escaping, the e-file being open!

(3) Black's Rook on d8 is guarding the d-pawn and the Rook on c8, and Black's pieces are over-stretched. Here is how White took advantage of that fact:

1 Bxf6! Bxf6 2 Nxd5! This move throws a spanner into the works again. Black dare not capture the Knight with his Bishop because of mate in two moves, starting with Qh7+, as we saw earlier. Nor can he move his Queen because White's Knight now controls e7, allowing (after, say 2 . . . Qb7) 3 Qh7+ Kf8 4 Qh8 mate. Finally, if Black plays 2 . . . Rxd5, White has 2 . . . Rxc8+ Bxc8 4 Re8 mate.

Before giving you some positions to think about for yourself, here is a

short game showing how a grandmaster will take full advantage of overworked pieces in the enemy camp. The White pieces were played by Tartakower in a simultaneous exhibition held in Paris in 1933. The opening is called a Giuoco Piano (Quiet Game!)

| 1 | e4 | e5 |
| 2 | Nf3 | Nc6 |
| 3 | Bc4 | Bc5 |
| 4 | d4 | exd4 |
| 5 | 0-0 | Nf6 |
| 6 | e5 | |

(beginning the dangerous 'Max Lange Attack')

| 6 | . . . | d5 |
| 7 | exf6 | dxc4 |
| 8 | Re1+ | Be6 |
| 9 | Ng5 | Qd5 |

(if 9 . . . Qxf6? 10 Nxe6 fxe6 11 Qh5+ – the double attack – and whatever Black replies, 12 Qxc5 wins a piece)

| 10 | Nc3 | Qf5 |

(not, of course, 10 . . . dxc3 which loses the Queen to 11 Qxd5 – Black's Bishop on e6 cannot recapture because it is pinned!)

| 11 | Nce4 | Bf8? |

(a mistake he should have played 11 . . . 0-0-0)

| 12 | Nxf7! | Kxf7 |
| 13 | Ng5+ | Kg8 |
| 14 | g4! | Qxf6 |

(not 14 . . . Qxg4? 15 Qxg4 Bxg4 16 f7 mate!)

| 15 | Rxe6 | Qd8 |
| 16 | Qf3 | Qd7. |

giving the following position:

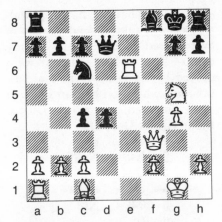

Diagram 23.5

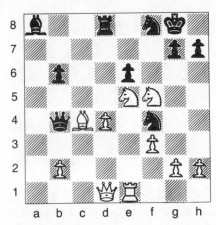

Diagram 23.6

Black's Queen now has to guard against Qf7 mate, and at the same time must watch over the d5 square. She is overworked, and it needs only 17 Re7!! to prove it. If now, 17 . . . Bxe7 the black Queen's defence of f7 is obstructed and White plays 18 Qf7 mate. if 17 . . . Qxe7 18 Qd5+ and Black can only interpose his Queen, delaying mate for just one move.

After Tartakower played **17 Re7**, the actual game ended **17 . . . Ne5 18 Rxe5 h6 19 Re7**! and here we are again with the same threats as before. Black had seen enough and promptly resigned.

Now, over to you. Set each one of these diagram positions up on your own board and really try hard to find the solutions before looking them up. Remember Bruce and the spider – 'If at first you don't succeed, try, try again.'

**Diagram 23.6** Eggenberger – Schumacher (Basle, 1959). White to move. Look at the black Queen. Which important square is she defending? How can you deflect her – and *why* should you deflect her?

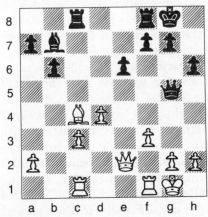

Diagram 23.7

**Diagram 23.7** Lilienthal – Tartakower (Paris, 1930). Black to move. Check what each white piece is doing and see if you can find any of them that are overworked. A clue: you 'only' win a pawn here.

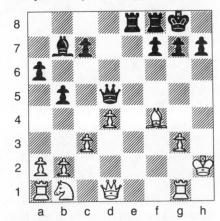

Diagram 23.8

**Diagram 23.8** Belenky – Pirogov (Moscow, 1957). Black to move. What is White's Queen preventing? Why must his Rook on g1 stay where it is? Find a move which throws a spanner into the works.

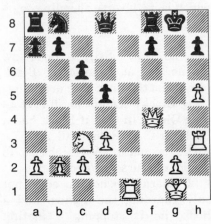

Diagram 23.9

*Diagram 23.9* Horwitz – Szen (London, 1851). White to move. He has Queen and two Rooks ready to attack the black King, while Black has only his Queen and a Rook to do any defending at the moment. White plays 1 Rg3+ Kh8 2 Qh6 Rg8. And now what? Prove that Black's pieces are overworked.

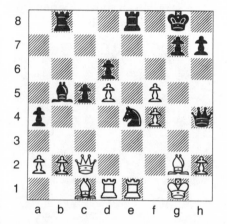

*Diagram 23.10*

*Diagram 23.10* Furman – Batugin (USSR). Black to move. White's Queen is guarding f2 and his Rook on d1 is protecting the other Rook. Does this give you an idea for a deflecting move? A clue: there's a fork at the end.

## Solutions

**Diagram 23.6**  The black Queen is preventing Ne7+ followed by Nf7 mate, so why not play a double attack by 1 Qd2!, winning at once? Black's Queen is threatened and he cannot move it without allowing the mate by the two Knights. Was it too easy for you? Did you think of 1 Qb3 as a way of deflecting Black's Queen? It does, but it also allows 1 ... Qxe1 mate.

**Diagram 23.7**  White's Queen is tied to the defence of his Bishop, his Rook on f1 is guarding the other Rook and his g-pawn is pinned by the black Queen. All this means that 1 ... Bxf3! wins a pawn. 2 Rxf3 allows 2 ... Qxcl+ while 2 Qxf3 would be followed by 2 ... Rxc4.

You may have thought that 1 ... Rxc4 was good, as it forces the white Queen to recapture, removing a defender from f3 and allowing 2 ... Bxf3, threatening mate with the Queen on g2. If 3 Rxf3 Qxcl+ and Black has still won a pawn. But White is *not* forced to play 3 Rxf3 to stop the mating threat. He could play the Rook on cl to c2, protecting the g2 pawn along the rank, and Black would have given up a Rook (5 points) for a Bishop and a pawn (total 4 points).

**Diagram 23.8**  White's Queen is stopping ... Qh5 mate, and his Rook is guarding against ... Qg2 mate. The 'spanner in the works' is 1 ... Re1! This Rook cannot be captured, for the reasons given, so White must play 2 Qg4. Black then has a choice between 2 ... Rxg1 3 Kxg1 Qg2 mate, and 2 ... Qh1+! 3 Rxh1 Rxh1 mate.

**Diagram 23.9**  After 1 Rg3+ Kh8 2 Qh6 Rg8, the black Rook is guarding against Qg7 mate and the black Queen is tied to f6 in order to prevent Qf6+ followed by mate. So once again it is a Rook that is flung in – 3 Re8! It cannot be captured because of the above mates. The game might end: 3 ... Qb6+ 4 Kh1 Nd7 5 Qg7 mate (Black's Rook is pinned!) but we'll also accept 5 Rgxg8 mate!

**Diagram 23.10**  Black throws a Bishop in this time. After 1 ... Bd3! 2 Qxd3 (2 Rxd3 Qxe1+) 2 ... Qf2+ 3 Khl Qxe1+ (did you see this?) 4 Rxe1 Nf2+ 5 Kgl Nxd3 and Black is the exchange up. Play may go on: 6 Rxe8+ Rxe8 7 Bd2 (or else Black plays 7 ... Re1 mate) 8 Nxb2 and Black will have very little trouble winning the ending.

# Unit 24

## The Back Rank Mate

After castling, we often try to keep the pawns in front of the castled King unmoved for as long as possible in order to give him protection. However, one of the greatest dangers then is the chance of a mate from an enemy Queen or Rook along an undefended back rank.

This mating idea usually involves overworked pieces and deflections, as you can see in the following position.

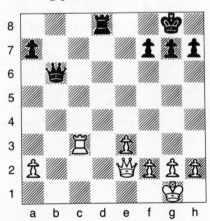

*Diagram 24.1*

*Diagram 24.1* Bernstein – Capablanca (Moscow 1914). Black has a Rook protecting his back rank (and ready to slam down to d1 and checkmate White if the white Queen should move away from protecting that square). White is probably hoping for an obvious move such as 1 ... Qb1+, when he can block this check by 2 Qf1. Then, if Black plays 2 ... Rd1? White could reply 3 Rc8+ and checkmate next move. (Try all these things out on your own board.)

But Capablanca is far too clever to fall for such an obvious trap. He finds a really brilliant move to deflect White's Queen from the protection of d1. See if you can find this move before you read on past the clue, which is: Black's move is a double attack and *must* win at least a Rook. Now, look and think.

Did you find it? The brilliant move was 1 ... Qb2!!, and if you found it – full marks to you. Can you see what it does? If White replies 2 Qxb2, Black mates with 2 ... Rd1. If White plays 2 Qe1, then Black wins by 2 ... Qxc3 after which 3 Qxc3, and here comes that old Rook mate on d1 again! So, as White could *not* play 3 Qxc3, he loses the Rook, leaving Black with an easy eventual win. This simple example shows us the dangers in leaving back ranks poorly defended and with no 'escape holes' for our King.

We must always be on guard against the possibility of being mated along the back rank — always making sure that our defences are sufficient.

Let us have a look at some more complicated examples than the one we have just shown you. Never be put off by what appear to be difficult positions. Just follow the main ideas, and you will soon learn that many positions that may *seem* complicated at first glance are really quite straightforward – when you know the 'tricks of the trade'.

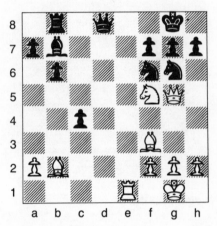

*Diagram 24.2*

*Diagram 24.2* Alekhine – Freeman (Blindfold Simultaneous Exhibition 1924). At the moment, Black's back rank is well defended by a Rook, the Queen and two Knights. That seems a good enough defence, doesn't it? But you will find it very instructive to see how Alekhine removes all these obstacles and checkmates with his Queen alone.

The first move is easy: 1 Bxb7 Rxb7, drawing the Rook away from the back rank with a straightforward exchange of pieces. Now comes 2 Bxf6 Qxf6, drawing the Queen away from the back rank. (Can you see why Black could not afford to play 2 ... gxf6? Work it out, remembering what we have said about deflection.) 3 Re8+ Nf8 is again easy to see, but what now? Well, look hard at Black's g-pawn. It is overworked (the old story) since it must guard the Queen *and* the h6 square at the same time. This means that after White plays 4 Nh6+!, Black must capture the Knight with his Queen. (The g-pawn is pinned, and if the King moves out of check to h8, Rxf8 mates.) So, after 4 ... Qxh6, Alekhine finishes things off very neatly with 5 Rxf8+ Kxf8 6 Qd8 mate.

A lovely series of moves, well worth playing through again. But it is not magic – just clear thinking.

The same can be said of the next position.

*Diagram 24.3* Stephenson – Blaine (Middlesex Championship 1962). This is an excellent example of deflection, easy to understand but not so easy to see over the board. By 1 Rd8+, White has deflected the Queen from protecting the e-pawn. 1 ... Qxd8 allows White to capture the e-pawn with 2 Qxe5 and threaten mate on g7. Black's only defence to that threat is Qd7, and now? Can you see White's back

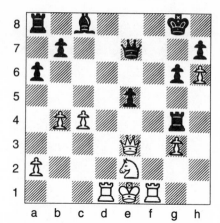

*Diagram 24.3*

rank mate idea? Work it out.

Our final example is just as complicated, but again you must follow the main ideas and not worry too much about details for now.

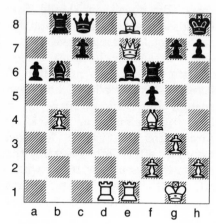

*Diagram 24.4*

*Diagram 24.4* Katalimov – Mnazakanian (USSR 1959). If Black did not have a Bishop on e6 and a Rook on f6, White could mate

in one by Qf8. Can we somehow deflect those two black pieces – give them other jobs to do that will take them away from their tasks of guarding the back rank?

As we shall see, the Bishop also has to protect d7 and the Rook has to keep his eyes on h6. As White now beautifully demonstrates, it is all too much.

1 Rd7! Bxd7 (2 Qxg7 mate was threatened, and 1 ... Qxd7 loses too much material.) 2 Bh6! Now, the threat is once again Qxg7 mate, and we see that not only the Rook but also the g-pawn is overworked. This poor little g-pawn has to guard the Rook as well as h6. Black resigned. What could he do? 2 ... Rxh6 allows 3 Qf8 mate, and after 2 ... gxh6, White has 3 Qxf6+ Kg8 4 Qf7+ Kh8 5 Qf8 mate.

Here is a short game that shows how back rank mating situations can come about in the first place. Weiss – Kupak (Zagreb 1928).

| | | |
|---|---|---|
| 1 | e4 | e5 |
| 2 | Nf3 | Nc6 |
| 3 | Bb5 | d6 |
| 4 | d4 | Bd7 |
| 5 | o-o | exd4 |
| 6 | Nxd4 | Nxd4 |
| 7 | Bxd7+ | Qxd7 |
| 8 | Qxd4 | Nf6 |
| 9 | Re1 | Be7 |
| 10 | e5 | dxe5 |
| 11 | Qxe5. | |

White thinks his attack on the black Bishop will stop Black castling, leaving the Bishop defended only by the Queen. But Black can even castle Queen side, as then 12 Qxe7 would lose to 12 ... Qxe7 13 Rxe7 Rd1 mate.

However, this would be too obvious and it is very doubtful if White would fall into such a trap, so Black plays a more cunning move, 11 ... o-o! As the Rook is not on an open file (as it would have been if Black had castled Queen side) and a back-rank mate does not seem so obvious now, White feels he can win the Bishop, so he plays 12 Qxe7? Black does *not* recapture. Instead he plays 12 ... Rfe8.

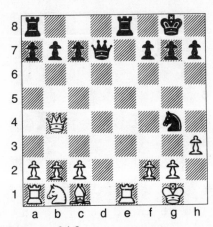

*Diagram 24.6*

*Diagram 24.6* This is the position Black had in mind when he castled King side. The white Queen is the only piece guarding the Rook on e1, and a back-rank mate is not far away. By now, you should find Black's idea easy to understand. He plays the deflecting move 14 ... Qd6 – attacking the white Queen *and* the h2 square – and after 15 Rxe8+ Rxe8 White has had enough and resigns. There is, in fact, no defence as Black is threatening 16 ... Qd1+ followed by mate after Qe1 (blocking the check) Qxe1 mate, or 16 ... Qh2+ Kf1 17 Qh1 mate. If White plays Qxd6 or Qxg4, Black has 16 ... Re1 mate.

Now it is your turn once again.

*Diagram 24.7* Capablanca – Fonarov (USA 1904). White to move. Can you think of a clever series of moves that wins material

*Diagram 24.7*

for White, based on the threat of a back-rank mate? Clue: Black's g-pawn is pinned – but protected.

*Diagram 24.5*

*Diagram 24.5* The back rank mate threat is back. Rather than lose his Queen, White withdraws 13 Qb4, guarding the Rook on e1. Now 13 ... Ng4 14 h3.

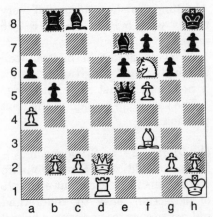

*Diagram 24.8*

*Diagram 24.8* Aitken – Payne (Whitby 1962). White to move and win. If you remember what we have told you about overworked pieces, then you should have no trouble here.

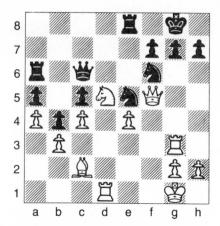

*Diagram 24.9*

*Diagram 24.9* Gragger – Dorn (Vienna 1958). White to move and win. You will enjoy this one but be careful! There are a number of tempting lines. Clue: There are two deflections in the main line.

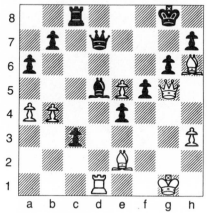

*Diagram 24.10*

*Diagram 24.10* Sämisch – Koch. White to move. We end up with a back-rank mate, but before that

there are two deflections. Here is some help: White's first move is 1 Rxd5! Can you see White's plan and how he achieves the back-rank mate? A clue: A pin comes into it as well as the two deflections.

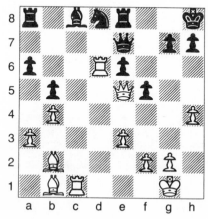

*Diagram 24.11*

*Diagram 24.11* Muffgang – Devos (Paris) White to move. He plays 1 Rc7!! What is his clever idea? Don't forget that the black Queen must never allow White to play Qxg7 mate.

## Solutions

Diagram 24.7 After 1 Nh6+ Kh8 (the g-pawn is pinned) 2 Qxe5! Qxe5 3 Nxf7+! White comes out a piece and two pawns up, since 3 . . . Rxf7? allows mate on the back rank. A nice mixture of the pin, the double attack, and the deflection.

Diagram 24.8 Did you find this

too easy? After 1 Qh6! threatening mate, Black has to capture the Knight, but his Bishop on e7 cannot possibly do all the work expected of him. If 1 . . . Bxf6, White has 2 Qf8 mate, and 1 . . . Qxf6 fails to 2 Rd8+! (deflection) 2 . . . Bxd8 (forced) 3 Qf8 mate. Simple, but very effective.

Diagram 24.9 1 Nxf6+ fails to 1 . . . Qxf6 and Black's Queen is guarded by the Rook on a6. You did very well if you saw 1 Ne7+! (removing the Rook from the back rank) 1 . . . Rxe7 2 Qxf6!! (this is the tricky one) 2 . . . Qxf6 3 Rd8+, followed by mate.

The only other way Black can stop the immediate mate is by playing 2 . . . Ng6, but then 3 Qxe7! (another deflection) 3 . . . Nxe7 4 Rd8+ mates again.

Diagram 24.10 After 1 Rxd5! Qxd5, White threatens Qg7 mate by playing 2 Qe7 (or Qf6) 2 . . . Qf7, when the whole point of the play is that 3 Bc4!! deflects either the Queen or the Rook. The two variations are: 3 . . . Qxc4 4 Qg7 mate, and 3 . . . Rxc4 4 Qd8+ Qf8 5 Qxf8 mate.

The keen ones among you may see that there are two other variations, depending upon whether White's Queen goes to e7 or f6 on move two. In the first case Black can play 2 . . . Qd4+ 3 Kh1, but then has no defence against the threat of

Qg7 mate. In the second case Black has 2 ... Qd7, but this loses to 3 Bc4+! Rxc4 4 Qf8 mate.

Diagram 24.11 Play goes 1 Rc7!! Qxc7 2 Rxd8! (the point) as now 2 ... Qxe5 allows 3 Rxe8 mate. 2 ... Qxd8 fails to 3 Qxg7 mate, and finally 2 ... Rxd8 leaves the Queen unprotected, so 3 Qxc7 wins it.

Note that, if White's h-pawn had been on h2 instead of h4, this last line would have won for Black as 3 Qxc7 then would have lost to 3 ... Rd1 mate!

# Unit 25

## More about Queen Endings

We have already seen how a pawn can promote to a Queen, and how a Queen can mate with the help of the King. In most pawn endings the side which can queen' first usually wins. Sometimes, therefore, we arrive at positions in which a Queen and King have to stop a pawn gaining promotion. Consider the first diagram:

*Diagram 25.1*

*Diagram 25.1* Black's pawn is about to promote so White must do something quickly. It does not take us long to see that there is no way of driving the black King away from his pawn. Try it and you will soon find out that, wherever we check him, he clings to his pawn and threatens to queen at every possible opportunity. For example: 1 Qe3+ Kd1 2 Qe4 Kc1 3 Qe3 Kc2 4 Qe4+ Kd1 5 Qc4 Ke1 and we are clearly making no progress.

But, if we look at these moves again, more carefully this time, we see that during that little sequence of moves White was twice given a 'breathing space' — when black was *not* threatening to promote. In other words there were two occasions when Black's King was blocking his own pawn, after 1 ... Kd1 and after 4 ... Kd1. Positions like this give White a chance to *bring his King into the action* and in fact win, as follows:

| | | |
|---|---|---|
| 1 | Qe3+ | Kd1 |
| 2 | Kg7! | Kc2 |
| 3 | Qe2 | Kc1 |

(not 3 ... Kc3 Qd1! when the pawn is no longer a threat)

| | | |
|---|---|---|
| 4 | Qc4+ | Kb2! |
| 5 | Qd3! | Kc1 |
| 6 | Qc3+ | Kd1 |
| 7 | Kf6 | |

(at last!)

| | | |
|---|---|---|
| 7 | ... | Ke2 |
| 8 | Qc2 | |

(playing the same manoeuvre as before but on the other side of the pawn)

| | | |
|---|---|---|
| 8 | ... | Ke1 |
| 9 | Qe4+ | Kf2! |
| 10 | Qd3! | Ke1 |
| 11 | Qe3+ | Kd1 |
| 12 | Ke5! | |

(edging nearer all the time)

| | | |
|---|---|---|
| 12 | ... | Kc2 |
| 13 | Qe2 | Kc1 |
| 14 | Qc4+ | Kb2! |
| 15 | Qd3! | Kc1 |
| 16 | Qc3+ | Kd1 |
| 17 | Ke4! | Ke2 |
| 18 | Qf3+! | |

(now the influence of White's King is felt)

| | | |
|---|---|---|
| 18 | ... | Ke1 |
| 19 | Ke3! | d1=Q |
| 20 | Qf2 mate (or 20 Qh1 mate) | |

All this takes quite a lot of time, and it may well annoy you that a little pawn can cause you so much trouble. But you can also think of it another way: if you have a *plan*, then every move you make is *progress*, even if it takes a lot of moves to carry out the whole of the plan!

It is the main idea that counts here, *to force your opponent's King to block his own pawn, allowing you to bring your King near enough to help.*

Now look at diagram 25.2.

*Diagram 25.2* At first sight there seems very little difference, but if we try the same plan as previously, after 1 Qb3+ Ka1 2 Kg7, it is Stalemate because there is no extra file available for the black King. The only way White can avoid this is to move his Queen away from the b-file, allowing 2 ... Kb1, threaten-

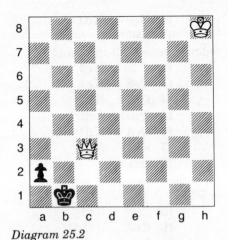

*Diagram 25.2*

ing to queen the pawn. So the game is drawn!

Now some questions for you:

(1) What would happen if Black had an extra pawn on a7 for instance? (see diagram 25.2 (a))

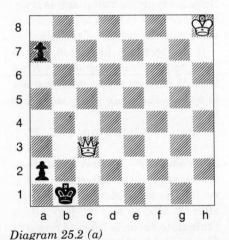

*Diagram 25.2 (a)*

(2) What would happen if White's King were on e1? (see diagram 25.3)

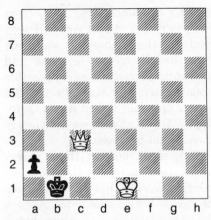

*Diagram 25.3*

(3) Go back to diagram 25.1 and move every piece one square to the left, as in diagram 25.4. We'll tell you at once that White cannot win this even if Black plays the best possible defence. Can you see how Black should go about securing a draw?

*Diagram 25.4*

Now consider the next position:

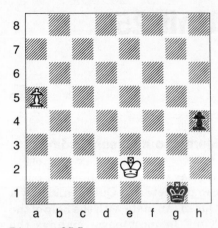

*Diagram 25.5*

*Diagram 25.5* Clearly each side wants to promote his pawn as quickly as possible, so **1 a6 h3 2 a7 h2 3 a8=Q h1=Q** would be the natural line to follow with White to play first. Now what? You could, of course, give the game up as a draw, but if you were White – with the move – you would probably want to try for a win. You need a *plan*. Based on what? A plan based on nothing is just a dream. White can give check and hope to improve the placing of his pieces. Let us try to bring the Queen nearer the scene of the action, being careful not to allow Black's Queen to interpose (with check!) drawing at once. So, let us continue:

    **4   Qa7+**

(*not* 4 Qg8+ Qg2+!)

| 4 | ... | Kh2 |
|---|---|---|
| 5 | Qc7+ | Kg2 |
| 6 | Qc6+ | Kg1 |
| 7 | Qc5+ | Kh2 |

```
8    Qe5+    Kg1
9    Qe3+    Kh2
10   Qf4+    Kh3
```

(already our position is much better, as 10 ... Kg1? would allow 11 Qf2 mate!)

```
11   Qh6+    Kg2
12   Qg5+    Kh3
13   Qh5+    Kg2
14   Qg4+    Kh2
```

leading to diagram 25.6.

*Diagram 25.6*

Note that there is no way Black could have avoided this position. In fact he has played the best defence and made White work hard to get what he wants. Now it's over to you again. How can White win?

*Diagram 25.7* You are Black and you have White's King in check. White's pawn is about to queen but is undefended at the moment. Can we do anything about it? If 1 Kg1

*Diagram 25.7*

then 1 ... Qa7+ wins the pawn at once, so **1 Kh2 Qb8+**, hoping for 2 Kg1? Qa7+, or 2 Kg2 Qb7+ (or 2 ... Qb2+) winning the pawn in either case. So White plays **2 Kh3!**, a good winning attempt because it now looks as though Black has nothing to do except resign gracefully. But there *is* a move for Black that

*Diagram 25.8*

draws! Find it, and think how lucky Black is that his King happens to be standing on a1.

*Diagram 25.9* For our next position, think back to when we told you that a Queen usually wins against a Rook, but that there can be problems!

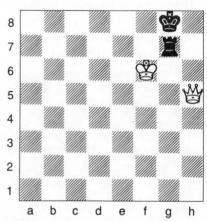

*Diagram 25.9*

As White, we have to find a way of winning from the position shown in diagram 25.9. Black has set up his strongest defensive position with his Rook clinging to the King for safety, and we would prefer it if it were Black to move from the diagram position. We can easily bring this about by 1 Qd5+ Kh7 2 Qh1+ Kg8 (not of course 2 ... Rh7 which allows 3 Qa8 mate!) 3 Qh5! Now we are back to the diagram position but with Black to move – and he is immediately in trouble! If now 3 ... Rh7 4 Qe8 is mate, and if 3 ... Kf8 4

Qh6 pins the Rook and wins it. So the black Rook must move away somewhere. Let's analyse what will happen after 3 . . . Rgl. We play 4 Qe8+ Kh7 5 Qd7+ Kg8 (not 5 . . . Kh6 6 Qh3 mate) 6 Qc8+ Kh7 7 Qc7+! Kg8 (if 7 . . . Kh8 8 Qh2+) 8 Qb8+ followed by 9 Qh2+ winning the Rook.

This is not as hard as it looks, but just to show that you understand White's plan, find how he wins after 3 . . . Ra7 (see diagram 25.10).

*Diagram 25.10*

## Solutions

**Diagram 25.2** (Question 1) Black does not want a pawn on a7 (as shown in diagram 25.2(a)) as he could then no longer escape by stalemate. White wins by 1 Qb3+ Ka1 2 Qc2! a5 (or a6) 3 Qc1 mate. If 1 . . . Kc1, then White captures both pawns and goes on to win.
(Question 2) White's King is near

enough to win by 1 Kd1! a1=Q 2 Qc2 mate. Although Black can stop this particular mate by promoting to a Knight instead of a Queen, White will win comfortably in the end. (Try it with a friend.)

**Diagram 25.4** (Question 3) If White tries the 'usual' winning plan of 1 Qd3+ Kc1 2 Kf7 Kb2 3 Qd2 Kb1 4 Qb4+ Ka2 5 Qc3 Kb1 6 Qb3+, Black does *not* play the apparently 'normal' 6 . . . Kc1? allowing White to play 7 Ke6, but has the clever resource 6 . . . Ka1! 7 Qxc2 is now forced to stop the pawn promoting. That would, of course, stalemate the black King. There is no way for White to win, as even if he carried on checking, the black King could always force this situation.

**Diagram 25.6** The winning move is 1 Kf2! giving a position which is very useful to remember. The black Queen cannot check without being lost, and White's Queen is threatening to mate on g3, h4 or h5. Black can stop the last of these by playing 1 . . . Qd5, but White then has either 2 Qh4 mate or 2 Qg3+ Kh1 3 Qgl mate. The only defence worth trying is the trap 1 . . . Qf3+ when of course you would not play 2 Qxf3? or would you?

**Diagram 25.8** Black could 'steal' a draw here by 1 . . . Qb3+! Now, if White moves his King out of check, his Queen is lost and so is the game,

so he has to settle for 2 Qxb3, leaving the black King without a legal move. Stalemate. You must always look for such possibilities when your position seems lost. You won't always find such a resource, but to avoid defeat, or even snatch a win, it is surely worth the trouble of looking hard before you give up.

**Diagram 25.10** Following the pattern we have already given you, the quickest way to win the Rook is 1 Qg4+ Kh8 (if 1 . . . Kf8? 2 Qc8 mates) 2 Qh3+ Kg8 (if 2 . . . Rh7? 3 Qc8 mates) 3 Qg3+! Kh7 (3 . . . Kh8 4 Qb8+, etc) 4 Qh2+ Kg8 5 Qb8+, and the Rook falls.

Finally, here is another possible way: 1 Qd5+ Kh8 2 Qd8+ Kh7 3 Qd3+ Kh8 (if 3 . . . Kh6? then Qh3 mates) 4 Qh3+ Kg8 (4 . . . Rh7? Qc8 mate) 5 Qb3+ Kh7 (5 . . . Kh8 6 Qb8+, etc.) 6 Qb1+! Kh8 7 Qb8+, winning the Rook. Easy, isn't it?

# Unit 26

## Unmasking Combinations

When we talked about the pin, we warned you not to pin without making sure that the pinned piece could not move away. In fact, this movement away of the pinned piece can be called 'unmasking' because it does indeed unmask the piece behind the pinned piece. The following combination will make this clear to you.

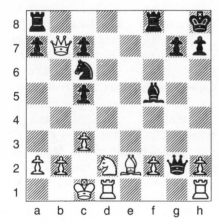

*Diagram 26.1*

*Diagram 26.1* Foldi – Florian (Budapest 1958). White's Queen is pinning the Knight, but if we look at it another way, it is White's Queen who is in danger if the Knight moves away. Problemists refer to Black's Queen and Knight as a 'battery'. In this case, the fire-power of the Queen is unmasked when the Knight moves away – provided the Knight can move to a square where he demands attention – leaving the Queen to make full use of her fire-power. Has the Knight a good square to go to? Of course, after 1 ... Nb4! 2 Qxg2 Nxa2 White is mated. Mate could only have been avoided by capturing the Knight which would have meant losing the Queen.

Look at this next position.

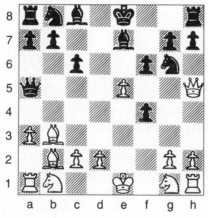

*Diagram 26.2*

*Diagram 26.2* Katalimov – Ilivitsky (Frunze 1959). Black's Queen is pinning the e-pawn right across the board, but once again we could look at it the other way about. If the pawn could move away with a good threat, then White's Queen would be attacking Black's! So White comes up with 1 Bf7+! Kxf7? 2 e6+ and the black Queen is lost. Even after the better reply 1 ... Kf8, White wins a piece with 2 Bxg6. Here's one more example of this type of escape from a pin.

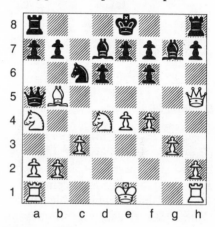

*Diagram 26.3*

*Diagram 26.3* Liebermann – Joffe (1961). White's Queen is not guarded, but neither is Black's! What about the black Knight on c6, you may ask. In fact, if there was no Bishop on d7, then Bxc6+ would remove the Knight, at the same time opening up the white Queen and Bishop battery to capture Black's Queen. All this gives White the clever idea of 1 Ne6!! (threatening the Bishop on g7) 1 ... Bxe6 (the f-pawn is pinned!) 2 Bxc6+ winning the Queen. Black saw this, so in the game he played 1 ... Bf8, but 2 b4! Nxb4 3 Bxd7+ still won the Queen. Now it's your turn.

*Diagram 26.4*

*Diagram 26.4* Haik – Derremeux (Bagneux 1970). White has just made the mistake of attacking Black's Queen by Re1, completely missing Black's reply, which is. . .? Clue: Has Black an unmasking move?

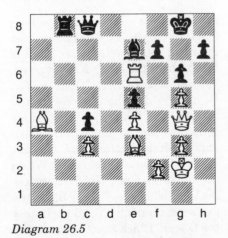

*Diagram 26.5*

*Diagram 26.5* Fischer – Shocron (Mar del Plata 1959). Black, a

Bishop down, has just played . . . Qc8 to win back his material by pinning White's Rook. However, Fischer had seen even further. What does he play? Clue: White wins a Queen for two pieces. Of course, a battery can be opened without a pin coming into it. The main point is that the unmasked piece needs something important to attack which forces the reply.

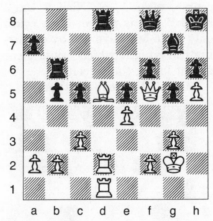

*Diagram 26.6*

*Diagram 26.6* Trifunović – Aaron (Beverwijk 1962). Black's Rook on d8 would be attacked with the white Bishop out of the way. All we have to do is find the most threatening square on which to place the Bishop. Can you see it? Do you remember the win that Marco missed against Von Popiel (diagram 21.5)? White plays 1 Bg8! threatening to checkmate on h7. Black can resign because he is forced to take the Bishop, and then White will

play 2 Rxd8 winning the black Queen. Devastating. This next unmasking combination is a little more complicated. It was played by a former World Champion.

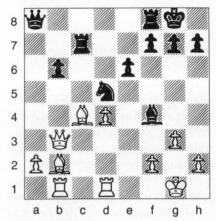

*Diagram 26.7*

*Diagram 26.7* Lissitsin – Smyslov (USSR 1944). Black has his eye on the e3 square, so he first plays 1 . . . Rxc4! 2 Qxc4 (removing White's Queen from where she can guard e3). Now all is set for the unmasking move 2 . . . Ne3! with the strongest of all threats – mate by . . . Qg2. White must take the Knight, but after 3 fxe3 Bxe3+ 4 Kf1 Qf3+, Black will mate next move.

Here is a short game played by the great Paul Morphy. With Black against Marache, Morphy produced the following gem, helped by some bad play from his opponent!

|   |      |        |
|---|------|--------|
| 1 | e4   | e5     |
| 2 | Nf3  | Nc6    |
| 3 | Bc4  | Bc5    |
| 4 | b4   |        |

(the Evans Gambit)

|   |      |        |
|---|------|--------|
| 4 | ...  | Bxb4   |
| 5 | c3   | Ba5    |
| 6 | d4   | exd4   |
| 7 | e5   |        |

(wasting valuable time)

|   |         |        |
|---|---------|--------|
| 7 | ...     | d5     |
| 8 | exd6e.p.| Qxd6   |
| 9 | 0-0     | Nge7   |
| 10| Ng5     | 0-0    |
| 11| Bd3     | Bf5    |

(White keeps moving his pieces to no effect instead of getting his Queen's-side pieces out. Meantime, Morphy calmly develops all his men.) **12 Bxf5 Nxf5 13 Ba3** (White goes for the win of material, but Morphy has seen it all and prepares an attractive finish).

|    |      |        |
|----|------|--------|
| 13 | ...  | Qg6    |
| 14 | Bxf8 | Qxg5   |

(all with gain of time)

|    |      |        |
|----|------|--------|
| 15 | Ba3  | dxc3   |
| 16 | Bc1  | Qg6    |
| 17 | Bf4  | Rd8    |
| 18 | Qc2  | Ncd4   |
| 19 | Qe4. |        |

Now, over to you. How did Morphy win from here?

*Diagram 26.8*

One final position for your enjoyment.

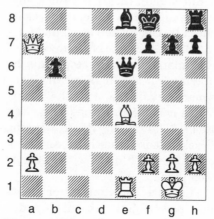
*Diagram 26.9*

*Diagram 26.9* Evans – Bisguier (USA 1958). White has a Rook and Bishop battery, but the Bishop cannot move at the moment because of ... Qxe1 mate. How does White manage to use an unmasking combination to win?

## Solutions

Diagram 26.4 The startling reply 1 ... Ne4!! closes one line and opens up another. White is lost because his Queen is attacked and 2 Qxe7 allows 2 ... Nd2 mate.

Diagram 26.5 Fischer plans to use an unmasking move by the Rook, so he plays 1 Bd7!! to remove the pin from his Rook. If now 1 ... Qxd7, Black's Queen is unguarded and 2 Rxg6+ wins her. Simple but effective.

Diagram 26.8 Once again an unmasking move by the Knight causes the damage, with an unguarded Queen the target. Morphy played 1 ... Ng3!! and it is all over because White's only way to save his Queen is 2 Qxg6 allowing 2 ... Nde2 mate. Lovely!

Diagram 26.9 Evans first played 1 Qa3+! forcing 1 ... Qe7 (because 1 ... Kg8 would allow 2 Bxh7+ winning the Queen), then play went on 2 Bc6! Qxa3 (Black's Queen is pinned!) 3 Rxe8 mate. So the target was not really Black's Queen, but his King!!!

# Unit 27

## Discovered Check

When a piece is unmasked so that it can attack the King we call it 'discovered check'. A good example is seen in the opening trap 1 e4 e5 2 Nf3 Nf6 3 Nxe5 Nxe4? 4 Qe2 Nf6?? 5 Nc6+ winning the black Queen for a Knight.

Note that White's Knight on e5 has a full choice of eight squares to which it can move, but of course he selects c6 attacking, and winning, the black Queen.

This ability of the unmasking piece to attack another piece without placing itself in danger is the strongest element in discovered check as can be seen in our next example.

*Diagram 27.1* Kan – Simagin (USSR, 1952). You may think the winning idea is simple, but in the actual game White missed it! Perhaps he saw that 1 Bh3+ fails because the black Rook captures the Bishop with check, but he did not realize that he can first play 1 Rd8+! Rxd8 and only then 2 Bh3+ Rd7 (the only move to stop mate immediately), 3 Rxd7!! setting up a

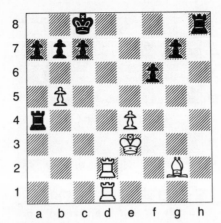

*Diagram 27.1*

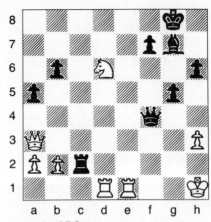

*Diagram 27.2*

winning battery. Try it for yourself and you'll see that Black is helpless. White's main threat is 4 Rook anywhere along the d-file, discovering check by the Bishop at h3 and forcing Black's King to b8, followed by 5 Rd8 mate. If Black stops this by playing 3 . . . b6, making an escape square available for the King, White can use his second threat of 4 Rd4+ followed by Rxa4, winning Black's Rook for nothing, and obviously leaving himself with an easily won game.

This excellent illustration shows how powerful the threat of a discovered check can be. The Rook, in this example, can choose almost any square it wants as there is no risk of being captured – Black's first problem being to get out of check, of course. Now, let's go back to the Knight as the unmasking piece – the nimble Knight which once again lives up to his name.

*Diagram 27.2* Vidmar – Euwe (Karlovy Vary 1929). Euwe is threatening . . . Qh2 mate, so Vidmar must act quickly – and positively. He probably sees at once the idea of 1 Re8+ Bf8 (if 1 . . . Kh7, White wins the Rook by 2 Qd3+) 2 Rxf8+! Kxf8, with a Queen and Knight battery. But how can he make the most of the discovered check? Where can the Knight go to to cause the most damage? White may have seen next that 3 Nf5+! looks strong, because if Black's Queen interposes on b4, White has Rd8 mate. But what is to be done after 3 . . . Kg8, when the black King threatens to escape to h7? We're not going to tell you what Vidmar played on move 4. Work it out for yourself.

Now another position for you to solve.

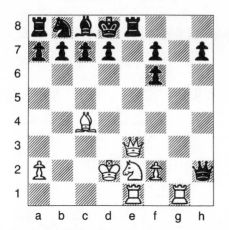

*Diagram 27.3*

Diagram 27.3 Perlasco – Grassi (Como 1907). We'll start you off – 1 Qxe8+! Kxe8, and White has set up the chance of a discovered check by the Knight. But to which square should the Knight move, and how does White follow up?

In our final test we give you a very useful clue.

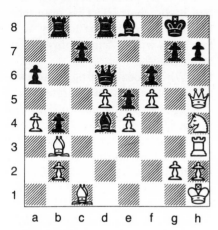

*Diagram 27.4*

*Diagram 27.4* Ahues – Ljubitel (Berlin 1932). There are *two* discovered checks in White's combination, the second one mating! How did White win? Black's King is cramped and you can surely see the unmasking possibility for White on the h-file. Do not miss White's fourth move – it is the whole point of the combination.

It is clear from all we have said above that the discovered check is a strong weapon to use against the enemy, but we now come to possibly *the* most powerful weapon in the game of chess. Suppose the unmasking piece in a battery gives check itself – *as well as uncovering a check from the masked piece!* We then have the dreaded 'double check', which can be deadly.

To show the double check at work, let's begin with a short game won by Nimzowitch with the white pieces:

| 1 | e4 | e5 |
|---|-----|------|
| 2 | Nf3 | Nc6 |
| 3 | Bb5 | Nf6 |
| 4 | 0-0 | d6 |
| 5 | d4 | Nxe4? |
| 6 | d5 | a6 |

(breaking the pin by the Bishop, since if 7 Ba4, Black has 7 . . . b5, but White's next move leaves both Knights attacked). **7 Bd3! Nf6 8 dxc6 e4** (double attack!) **9 Re1** (a pin counters the double attack) **9 . . . d5 10 Be2** (10 Bf1 would be perfectly good, but White sets an amus-

ing trap based on the double check weapon). **10 . . . exf3 11 cxb7 Bxb7** (after 11 . . . fxe2 12 bxc8=Q, the e-pawn is pinned! **12 Bb5 double checkmate**. This final position is worth a diagram (27.5).

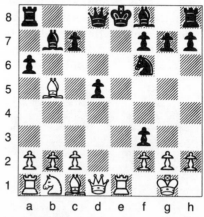

*Diagram 27.5*

This picture tells the story without need of words. There are three ways a King can escape a normal check as you will doubtless remember from Unit 6, but when we give double check *the King is forced to move*, and the other two possibilities are denied him. In the above diagram, if it were just the Rook giving check, Black could play . . . Be7, and if it were the Bishop only giving check, Black could play . . . axb5. But in this example, both pieces checking together give mate as Black's King has nowhere to go, and capturing one of the attacking pieces or blocking one of the checks is not enough. The other check is still there.

Double check can be so devastating that it is often well worth sacrificing material in order to bring it about. Once the student realizes this he will soon understand the most complicated-looking combinations. Let us examine some more positions, beginning with a justly famous combination created by Adolf Anderssen, the attacking genius of the nineteenth century.

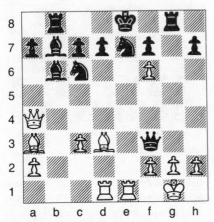

*Diagram 27.6*

*Diagram 27.6* Anderssen – Dufresne (Berlin 1852). White has already sacrificed two Knights for a pawn and he sacrifices even more material to bring about the position he wants. After 1 Rxe7+! Nxe7 2 Qxd7+!! Kxd7, the black King has been lured to a square which allows 3 Bf5++. If now 3 . . . Kc6 4 Bd7 mate, so Black plays 3 . . . Ke8, but is still mated by Bd7+ Kf8 5 Bxe7 mate.

It would be wrong to expect you to

find every move of such a combination – yet! But it shows that the brilliancies (like the mistakes) are all there waiting to be made, and your time could easily come.

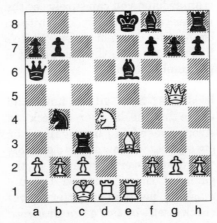

*Diagram 27.7*

*Diagram 27.7* Borich – Osmolovsky (Moscow 1953). This is a splendid example of two batteries at work. First of all comes the sacrifice 1 Qd8+! Kxd8 which brings Black's King in line for 2 Nxe6++, As 2 . . . Kc8 allows 3 Rd8 mate, Black plays 2 . . . Ke7. It is now we can see how cleverly White has worked it all out. By 3 Bg5+! f6, he stops Black's King escaping to f6, gives him the f7 square, then immediately takes it away again by 4 Nd8+! Qe6 5 Rxe6 mate. A question for you: What would White have played against 2 . . . Ke8.?

Surely you are convinced by now of the tremendous power of the double check. Just in case you are

not, here's a final example you won't forget in a hurry.

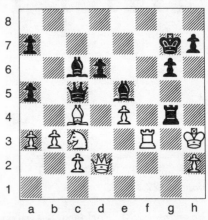

*Diagram 27.8*

*Diagram 27.8* Bitman – Alexeyev (Moscow 1969). White is threatening Rf7+ followed by Qh6 and a quick mate. Black stops this at once by 1 . . . Qxc4!! but why can he do this? Because after 2 bxc4 Bd7!! White is helpless against the Rook and Bishop battery! This may seem incredible, but it is true. Try out a few lines with a friend playing the other pieces.

If White does nothing, Black will simply play 3 . . . h6! followed by 4 . . . Rg3++ 5 Kh4 g5+ 6 Kh5 Bg4 mate. White can give up his Rook by 3 Rf5, but after 3 . . . gxf5 he is still lost. His best chance is probably 3 Qf2 Rg3++ 4 Kh4 g5+ 5 Kh5 Be8+ 6 Rf7+ Bxf7+ 7 Qxf7+ Kxf7 8 hxg3 Bxc3, but Black still wins.

In the actual game, White did not capture the black Queen, but after 2

Kxg4 Qe6+ 3 Kh4 h6! he had to resign.

Now, a question for you: in the diagram position a German chess player found a different way of winning for Black by using the double attack weapon (not double check). Can you spot the winning move the German player found?

Finally, while you're feeling sharp and 'tuned in' to this sort of attack, here are three more positions for you to solve.

*Diagram 27.9* Charousek – Wollner (Kaschau 1893). White to play and win. Clue: can you somehow use that pawn on f7?

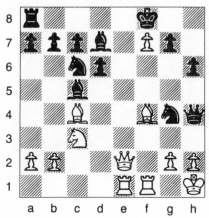

*Diagram 27.9*

*Diagram 27.10* Jerostrom – Bergman (Ljusdal 1950). White to play. Can you bring about a winning double check?

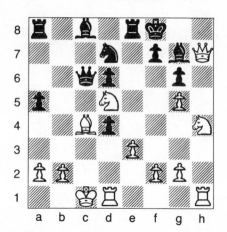

*Diagram 27.10*

*Diagram 27.11* A 'constructed' position. You are White. You have lost a lot of material and you cannot even win the black Queen by 1

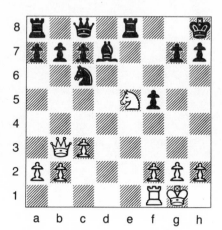

*Diagram 27.11*

Nf7+ Kg8 2 Nd6+, because of 2 ... Be6, attacking *your* Queen. How can the magic of the double check save you?

## Solutions

Diagram 27.2 Vidmar lured Black's King back to f8 by 4 Qf8+ Kxf8 5 Rd8 mate. (Had Black played 4 ... Kh7, then 5 Qg7 mates.)

Diagram 27.3 White mustn't play 1 Rg8+ when Black's King will escape to d6, but he can first play 2 Nd4+! Kf8 3 Re8+! Kxe8, and *then* 4 Rg8+ Ke7 5 Nf5 mate.

Diagram 27.4 Ahues won by 1 Qxh7+! Kxh7 2 Ng6+ Kg8 3 Rh8+ Kf7 4 Rf8+ (the whole point) Qxf8 5 d6 mate.

Diagram 27.7 After 1 Qd8+! Kxd8 2 Nxe6++, if Black plays 2 ... Ke8, White has 3 Nxg7+ Bxg7 4 Bg5+ followed by 5 Rd8 mate. If Black played, on move 3 ... Ke7, White can *double checkmate* by 4 Bg5!

Diagram 27.8 The German player discovered that another very direct and simple win was possible after 1 ... Bf4! When the threat of ... Qh5 mate wins lots of material for Black.

Diagram 27.9 White has a forced mate by 1 Qe8+! Rxe8 2 fxe8=Q+ Bxe8 3 Bxd6 double checkmate!

Diagram 27.10 After 1 Nxg6+! fxg6 2 Qg8+! Kxg8 White has set up a winning double check by 3 Ne7++. Although the Bishop and Knight are both attacked, their double check forces 3 ... Kf8 4 Nxg6 mate.

Diagram 27.11 We hope you haven't looked up this solution before trying to solve the combination for yourself. We would not blame you if you took a draw by perpetual check with 1 Nf7+ Kg8 2 Nh6++ Kh8 3 Nf7+, etc., but there is a beautiful 'smothered' mate here. Full marks if you spotted it: 1 Nf7+ Kg8 2 Nh6++ Kh8 3 Qg8+!! Rxg8 4 Nf7 mate.

# Unit 28

## Starting the Game

Just look at this position.

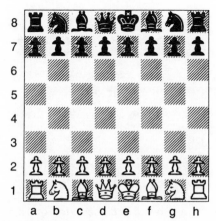

*Diagram 28.1*

Complicated isn't it? Well, you may not think it looks so frightening now that you have spent time studying the previous 27 Units, but perhaps you can remember what a hash you made of your game when you first started trying to play from this position.

At that time, with only a slight idea of the powers and limitations of the various pieces and pawns you must have made some terrible opening moves, reached some awful

positions, and been beaten almost before you had warmed your seat. You will undoubtedly have won some games quickly too, but probably more as a result of your opponent's bad play than of any plan of your own.

That sort of thing is inevitable when beginners try to play chess with a full set from the word go, and that is why we have brought you along gently – fully explaining each piece individually and giving examples of how to use pieces in harmony.

Now perhaps, you can see the reasoning behind all those exercises we set and all the practising we asked you to do.

If you practised properly you should be quite a reasonable end-game player by now, and as knowledge breeds confidence it will not worry you as your more powerful pieces are exchanged off during a game. *You* can use Kings and pawns well enough not to worry about reaching an end-game, but many players who have not learned these things so well are scared to death of endings – as you will see when you meet such players in competition.

You should also have a good idea of how to hold your own in the middle-game, and as you play more and more games you will add to your ability to pick your way through the often complicated situations that arise, and leave

yourself with what you know to be a favourable end-game position.

So now you need to learn how to open a chess game – soundly – and you will learn this much more easily because we have already given you a good working knowledge of your chess army's strengths and weaknesses, both as individual pieces and when they are operating in harmony with other pieces.

There are several 'rules' that apply to sound opening play. You must not waste moves; you must develop your pieces as quickly as possible to what you feel are the 'best' squares for them in relation to the type of opening you are playing; and you must ensure that your pieces command for you a fair share of the territory on which the battle is taking place.

But which pieces do we develop first? To which squares? In what order? It is not easy to answer these questions because there are no fixed answers. Much depends upon what you are trying to achieve and how far your opponent's moves go towards baulking your plans and ideas.

A chess game can open in many different ways. As White, the opening or type of opening you use will depend upon what type of game you prefer. Some players choose openings that will lead more quickly to a tactical type of game where there is lots of action with pieces flying around – capturing and recapturing

– and direct attacks on the opponent's King. Others prefer more strategical games with lots of manoeuvring while trying to outplay the opponent and gradually gaining a better position. Most games involve elements of both strategy and tactics, but in what proportions you prefer to use them is a highly personal thing, dictated by the kind of position reached from the opening.

For fun, play a few opening moves against a friend with one of you moving nothing but pawns. It won't be long before you realize the uselessness of moving pawns for no particular reason – especially if one of you achieves one of the quickest mates possible, like 1 f4 e6 2 g4?? Qh4 mate!

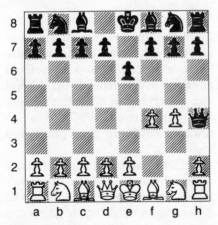

*Diagram 28.2*

The player moving only pawns will soon find himself in hopeless positions as his opponent develops pieces, tucks away his King, and attacks.

Of course, we can't move our Bishops or the Queens or Rooks until we have moved some pawns out of the way, but we need to use a mixture of piece and pawn moves in order to achieve balanced development without loss of time.

When making pawn moves remember what we have told you in earlier Units about how valuable these little fellows are. Remember too that once you move a pawn he cannot move back again. If you bear those points in mind you will naturally move them sensibly.

Pawns in the opening can, and do, provide valuable support for pieces. Take the Knight for example. He is the only piece that can get into play before even one pawn is moved, but he can find himself in deep trouble if he wanders about without help.

A famous American grandmaster, Reuben Fine, found this to his cost in the following game with the black pieces against Borochov.

Fine chose to play an opening called Alekhine's Defence, but he played it badly. Remember that Alekhine's Defence is one opening in which a player allows his opponent to force him to move the same piece more than once (violating one of the 'rules'). In Alekhine's Defence, Black's idea is to place the Knight in tantalizing positions and lure on White's pawns to attack

him. Then he moves away, hopefully leaving White with an overstretched pawn structure. Played properly it can be a very useful defence, but there is no margin for error.

The Borochov – Fine game started like this:
**1 e4 Nf6 2 e5 Nd5 3 c4 Nb6 4 d4 Nc6?** (4 . . . d6 should be played here) **5 d5 Nxe5 6 c5! Nbc4 7 f4.**

*Diagram 28.3*

Black has done it all wrong and with no support from the pawns one of his Knights is lost. Even if he had played differently on move 5 he would still find trouble because of this lack of support.

For example, 5 . . . Nb4 6 c5! Nbxd5 7 a3. See diagram 28.4.
Or 5 . . . Na5 6 c5 Nbc4 7 b4. See diagram 28.5.

You may well be wondering how a

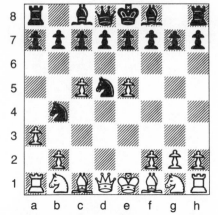

*Diagram 28.4*

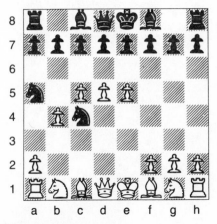

*Diagram 28.5*

grandmaster can get himself into such a terrible position so early in a game, especially in a well-established opening he must have known for years. How can a grand-master make such an elementary mistake as to leave his Knights unsupported? Well, we don't know for sure, but a fair guess would be that Fine thought he had found something new in this opening that he could spring on his unsuspecting opponent, but once he started to play it he realized it had shortcomings. Chess players are constantly trying to find 'new' moves in well-known positions – and such moves don't always work. Once you understand chess better you should also be seeking surprise moves, but try to make sure they are sound and do not violate any of the 'rules' unless you are convinced the rewards are there for you.

Here is another example from an Alekhine's Defence opening:
**1 e4 Nf6 2 e5 Ne4? 3 d3 Nc5 4 d4 Ne6** (if 4 . . . Ne4?, 5 f3 wins the Knight) **5 d5 Nc5 6 Be3 Na4?** (6 . . . e6 would certainly have been better).

*Diagram 28.6* How does White win the Knight?

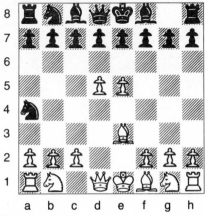

*Diagram 28.6*

These examples clearly show the danger of moving Knights about the board without some support from the pawns. Normally at least one pawn move is needed to give pieces some sort of a foothold.

This is why 1 e4 is such a popular opening move for White. It enables the King's Knight to be developed to f3 without the danger of later being driven away by Black playing a pawn to e4, and it gives the King's Bishop a chance to settle on c4, for instance, without the danger of . . . d5 driving him away immediately. With these two pieces satisfactorily developed White can castle as soon as he likes, tucking his King away and bringing a Rook nearer the centre.

At the same time it is wrong to overdo the pawn moves in the open-ing stages for while we are spending time pushing pawns our opponent will be developing pieces and establishing them in good positions ready to attack before we get our own pieces into play. We must not lose time at any stage of the game and certainly not in the opening.

Time in chess is called 'tempo'. A move is a tempo. More than one move – tempi. If White loses a tempo in the opening he loses the benefit of having first move, allow-ing Black to 'equalize'. If Black loses a tempo he is often struggling.

We have used examples of Alekhine's Defence because it shows a number of the points we

*Diagram 28.7*

| 2 | e5 | Nd5 |
|---|-----|------|
| 3 | c4 | Nb6 |
| 4 | d4 | d6 |
| 5 | f4 | dxe5 |
| 6 | fxe5 | Nc6 |
| 7 | Be3 | Bf5 |
| 8 | Nc3 | e6 |
| 9 | Nf3. | |

Now Black can try any of the following moves: 9 ... Qd7, 9 ... Nb4, 9 ... Be7 or 9 ... Bg4. These are all well-known continuations, but if you want to try other moves here please do so. The more things you discover for yourself the quicker you will learn.

### Solution

Diagram 28.6 White wins the Knight by 7 c4 Nb6 8 c5, or if 7 ... b5, 8 b3! Nb6 9 c5, with the same result.

wanted to drive home to you early. However, although our examples show Black as the sufferer do not let them turn you away from playing this defence.

Correctly employed it can be a very useful defence for Black, and while it is not often played at grandmaster level now, you can still win games with it at your own level.

If you would like to see how Alekhine's Defence leaves both sides after nine moves without any silly mistakes by either side, here is an example of the Four Pawns' Attack variation – probably White's most violent attempt at refuting Black's plans.

Play the moves to the diagram position and then see if you or your opponent can best exploit the position. Take your turns with the White and Black pieces.

| 1 | e4 | Nf6 |
|---|-----|------|

# Unit 29

## The Queen in the Opening

The basics of opening play can be summed up in three words – time, space and force.

TIME (Tempo): Make every move count and think carefully before committing yourself.

SPACE: Ensure you develop each pawn and piece to a square that gives maximum control of as much territory as possible, and from which it cannot easily be driven away. Do not forget to give your pieces ample support and place them where they can be ready to work with other pieces as they are developed.

FORCE: Develop as many pieces as quickly as possible so you can either threaten to attack when you are ready, or be in a position to repel the enemy's pieces should he attack first.

The reference to 'force' may start you thinking how you can get your more powerful pieces into play, but that is not what is meant. It is the number of pieces you can use in harmony that counts, not, for instance, getting the 'all-powerful' Queen into the battle too soon. This

can be, and often is, disastrous. Look at this opening sequence for example:

**1 e4 e5 2 Qg4? Nf6 3 Qh3? d5 4 Qf3? dxe4**

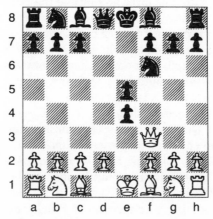

*Diagram 29.1*

White's stupid Queen moves have lost not only a good pawn but several tempi as well. Furthermore, you can be sure his Queen will be subjected to more pressure before long, causing further loss of time.

Even if White should see the danger signs now and take the Queen back 'home' (to d1) Black would simply develop another piece and have *two* pieces in play while White has nothing in the field.

The Queen is so powerful that the beginner is often tempted to bring her into action much too early. However, her very strength can work against her because she is practically *forced* to move when attacked. Always remember that

even the Queen can do little on her own against a well-defended enemy position, especially when the enemy has developed properly and his pieces can work in harmony.

In this next example the Black pieces were played by a beginner who honestly thought he was doing the right things.

**1 e4 d5** The 'Centre Counter', a risky opening. **2 exd5 Qxd5** As a result of this move Black now begins to lose tempi. **3 Nc3**, attacking the Queen while developing a piece. Sound thinking by White, but if Black had played 3 . . . Qd8, or 3 . . . Qa5, he could perhaps have survived. But he didn't play carefully. He had probably heard one of the silly pieces of 'advice' often given to beginners: 'Never miss a check, it might be mate'. Well, he checked: **3 . . . Qe5+? 4 Be2.** (Black had even encouraged White to develop a piece here) **4 . . . Bg4 5 d4 Bxe2.**

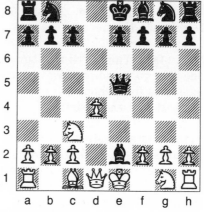

*Diagram 29.2*

Black probably thought that as his Queen was attacked he would attack White's Queen, but all he really achieves is to help White develop yet another piece. **6 Ngxe2**, and Black has to move his threatened Queen – again.

**6 ... Qd6? 7 Bf4 Qb6 8 Nd5** The position gets worse, but Black can see another check!

**8 ... Qa5+** (What satisfaction!)

**9 Nec3 a6? 10 b4!** Now where will the all-powerful Queen go?

*Diagram 29.3*

**10 ... Qa3**. This is the only square she *can* go to while awaiting the axeman's final chop.

**11 Bc1!** And that's that.

In the next example it is White who commits his Queen early, and suffers accordingly by trying to keep her in play once she has done the job he brought her out to do.

**1 e4 e5 2 d4 exd4 3 Qxd4** All right

up to now – this opening is known as the Centre Game which was popular a long time ago. There are things to recommend it but generally it gives Black so much time, space *and* force advantage that the opening is not played very often nowadays. Black of course develops a piece and attacks the Queen by **3 ... Nc6**. The normal move now for White would be 4 Qe3, but White, probably reluctant to 'retreat' advances instead.

**4 Qd5?** (So many beginners – and even some experienced players – seem to think that to retreat is a loss of face. It certainly need not be. If you don't like the word 'retreat' call it 'reorganization') Black now gains more time.

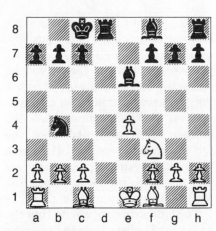

*Diagram 29.4*

| 4 | ... | Nf6 |
|---|-----|-----|
| 5 | Qc4 | Qe7 |
| 6 | Nc3 | d5! |
| 7 | Nxd5 | Nxd5 |

| 8 | Qxd5 | Be6 |
|---|------|-----|
| 9 | Qb5 | 0-0-0 |
| 10 | Nf3 | Qb4+ |
| 11 | Qxb4 | Nxb4 |

and White is in a lot of trouble. See diagram 29.4.

After 12 Bd3, Black can win back his pawn at once by 12 ... Nxd3+ 13 cxd3 Rxd3, or he can play more cleverly by 12 ... Rxd3! 13 cxd3 Nc2+ 14 Kd1 Nxa1 15 b3 Nxb3 16 axb3 Bxb3+ with a winning endgame. Notice how quickly openings can sometimes turn into endgames.

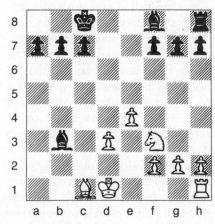

*Diagram 29.5*

Now we give an example where it almost appears as though White was trying to lose as quickly as possible! **1 e3 e5 2 Qf3? d5 3 Nc3 e4 4 Qf4? Bd6**.

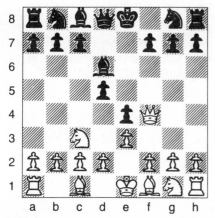

*Diagram 29.6*

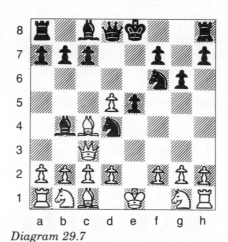

*Diagram 29.7*

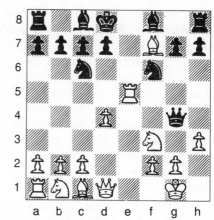

*Diagram 29.8*

The Queen is trapped in the middle of the board after only four moves and has nowhere to go. Believe it or not, this was an actual game: Spiel – Künzel!

Now look at this one:

| 1 | e4 | e5 |
|---|-----|------|
| 2 | Bc4 | Nc6 |
| 3 | Qh5? | g6 |
| 4 | Qf3? | Nf6 |
| 5 | Qb3? | d5 |
| 6 | exd5 | Nd4 |
| 7 | Qc3? | Bb4! |

(See diagram 29.7.)
White has wasted far too much time with these ridiculous Queen moves and now he has to pay for it. He must lose material since 8 Qxb4 allows the reply 8 ... Nxc2+ forking King and Queen (and the Rook on a1 for good measure!). If White saw that coming and played instead 8 Qd3? the reply 8 ... Bf5 is also crushing.

Black's turn this time to misuse his Queen – and suffer for it.
**1 e4 e5 2 Nf3 Qf6? 3 Bc4 Qg6 4 0-0 Qxe4?** Not only has Black brought the Queen out too early, but he is wasting time by moving her about too much when not forced to do so. **5 Bxf7+! Kd8** (if the King captures the Bishop, White has Ng5+ forking King and Queen). **6 Re1 Qg4 7 Rxe5 Nf6** (not 7 ... Nc6?? which allows an immediate mate by 8 Re8) **8 d4 Nc6 9 h3,** and again – a dead Queen! See diagram 29.8.

You are probably thinking that players who use their Queens so irresponsibly are few and far between, but just look around when you see a group of beginners playing (or cast your mind back to some of your own early mistakes!).

Sometimes, when one beginner brings out his Queen early in the game, his opponent (if he too is

fairly new to the game) gets worried, thinking that, faced with such power, he is in trouble. You should be hoping to meet a player who tries these early Queen attacks against you. If you just keep your head you can usually chalk up another win. But, be warned! Just because we have shown you that early Queen attacks usually rebound against the attacker, do not get careless if and when you do meet such an attack. You know it can't be good play by your opponent, but you must be sure you play sensibly against it. Do not get lured into chasing the Queen unless you have worked out how you can win it. You could easily neglect your own proper development and find yourself in a bad position by chasing for chasing's sake. First, have a good look to make sure the enemy Queen is not threatening anything – either immediately or if another piece were brought out in support. Then do what you think is best. If you *know* you can capture the Queen, or if you can attack her while developing your own pieces sensibly, fine, but don't get caught like Black did here after the moves 1 e4 e5 2 Bc4 Bc5 3 Qf3 Ne7?? We won't give a diagram. Look at it on your own board. This and similar disasters have happened early in many chess games, and they could happen to you! You may be feeling nervous; the game has only just started; you have not yet settled down to the game; the butterflies in your tummy are making the early moves – so it is surprising what you can overlook.

Here is an example to show just what we mean about keeping your head. Black's Queen is in action too early but White doesn't go mad with his moves. He develops smoothly and properly while at the same time making things uncomfortable for the black Queen.

| 1 | e4 | d5 |
|---|------|-------|
| 2 | exd5 | Qxd5 |
| 3 | Nc3 | Qg5? |
| 4 | Nf3 | Qc5? |
| 5 | d4 | Qd6 |
| 6 | Nb5. | |

All White's moves have gained time and space. His development is fine – even moving his Queen's Knight twice is acceptable because he is now threatening to capture Black's Queen thus gaining more time.

**6 . . . Qe6+ 7 Be3 Na6** (preventing Nxc7+, winning the black Queen but placing the Knight at the edge of the board where his power is halved).
**8 d5 Qe4 9 Nc3 Qg6 10 Bb5+ Kd8**, (if 10 . . . Bd7, then 11 Bxd7+ Kxd7 12 Ne5+ wins the Queen).
**11 Ne5 Qf5 12 f4 Nh6.**

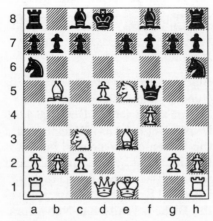

*Diagram 29.9*

Over to you. Can you find a way White can win at least a piece for a pawn in the next few moves? Remember what you have learned about double attacks and deflections.

### Solution

Diagram 29.9 White wins the Knight for a pawn by playing 13 g4! Nxg4 (Qf6 allows 14 g5, forking Queen and Knight) 14 Qxg4! (Did you see this 'deflection' idea?) and

White has won this Knight for the pawn. The black Queen cannot recapture because she would leave the f7 square unguarded for White to play 15 Nxf7 mate!

# Unit 30

## More about Opening Play

Like the Queen, Rooks are far too valuable to move into the enemy camp early in the game, with very rare exceptions.

It is difficult in any case to bring out the Rook very early because at least a Knight and a Bishop (and therefore a pawn, too) must move before castling can take place bringing the Rook into play. If Queen's side castling is desired, then the Queen herself must also move out of the way first.

You must also learn that developing the Rook along the a-file or the h-file, by first moving the appropriate pawn early on, very rarely pays dividends, and usually loses tempi or even material.

Why? Because the Rook is so easily attacked by the minor pieces and pawns – as can be seen from the following example:

**1 e4 h5? 2 Nf3 Rh6?? 3 d4 Rb6? 4 Nc3 e6** (see diagram 30.1).

Black's Rook does not look at all happy out in the open all on his own. He may be a force to be reckoned with when he is used properly, but here he is very vulnerable indeed.

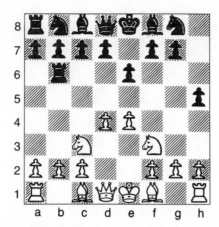

*Diagram 30.1*

See if you can win the exchange here for White.

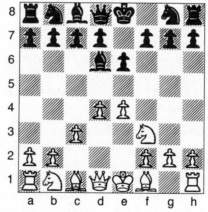

*Diagram 30.2*

The position in diagram 30.2 came about because Black made some thoughtless Bishop moves. The game started:

**1 e4 e6 2 Nf3 Bc5? 3 d4 Bb4+ 4 c3 Bd6?** This is really bad, blocking-in his own d-pawn. Black should have

seen that 2 ... Bc5 could be driven away by 3 d4 (as actually happened in the game) and that the check on move 3 could also be blocked by a pawn, which in the process of blocking the check also attacked the Bishop, forcing him to move yet again. So all this to-ing and fro-ing on the f8-a3 diagonal was a complete waste of time.

**5 Bd3**. Now White can castle whenever he likes and if Black tries to develop his King's Knight to either e7 or f6 he loses a piece to 6 e5!

When you have finished with the previous exercise, set up your board again and we will show you an example of poor opening play by White.

**1 e4 e5 2 Nf3 Nc6 3 Bc4 Bc5 4 d3 Nf6**. Reasonable enough so far, but now **5 Ng5?** and White has committed what is a common error among beginners by starting an attack

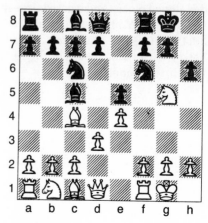

*Diagram 30.3*

much too soon, and in the process helps Black to gain tempi by **5 . . . 0–0 6 0–0 h6**. See diagram 30.3.

When he played 5 Ng5, White was probably thinking that this move attacks the pawn on f7 twice while it is defended only by the King – which is no defence at all really since, if the f7 pawn were captured either by the Knight or by the Bishop, the King could not recapture as he would be moving into check from the second attacking piece. But, of course, by castling Black developed his Rook to where it could defend the f-pawn and he could then, with **6 . . . h6**, put the Knight under direct attack. Play continued: **7 Nxf7? Rxf7 8 Bxf7+ Kxf7** White has gained a Rook and pawn for his Knight and Bishop (6 points for 6 on the approximate scale of values given in Unit 14), but in so doing he has also exchanged off his only two developed pieces and wasted time in the process. You can see in diagram 30.4 that Black definitely stands better with three pieces in the field to White's none.

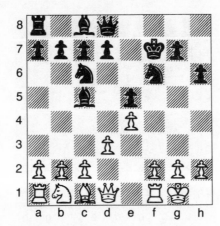

*Diagram 30.4*

The fact that Black has a slightly 'draughty' haven for his King is of little consequence as it is Black who will be dictating the future course of the game, keeping White under such pressure that his King is unlikely to be seriously threatened. Try out this position with a friend, playing it first as Black and then as White.

Here is a game from master chess (Botvinnik – Spielmann), in which Black was severely punished for trying a Queen attack far too soon. He should have known better.
**1 e4 c6 2 c4 d5 3 exd5 cxd5 4 d4 Nf6 5 Nc3 Nc6 6 Bg5 Qb6 7 cxd5 Qxb2? 8 Rc1 Nb4**

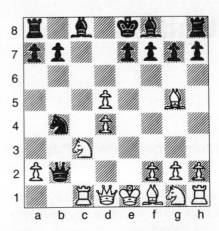

*Diagram 30.5*

Spielmann, who has played so many wonderful combinations himself, now has to lose a piece in order to save his Queen.

How did Botvinnik bring this about?

We have shown you that mistakes can be made in chess by beginners and by grandmasters. Although we have pointed out some of the possible places where you can go wrong, and warned you and given you advice, you too will make mistakes as you play more chess. Everyone does. But it is a near-truth to say that a game of chess is won by the player who made the *last-but-one* mistake!

So never get upset when you go wrong somewhere along the tricky chess road. Learn from your mistakes and try not to repeat them. After all, both sides start a game with equal forces and playing under the same laws. Therefore, it is reasonable to say that, if neither player made a mistake, every game would end in a draw!

Because of this equal start, a very early attack will have little chance of succeeding as the attacker has no more pieces available for attack than his opponent has for defence. That is provided the defender himself has developed soundly and plays sensibly against the sudden onslaught. But of course, not everyone plays sensibly. Take this example:

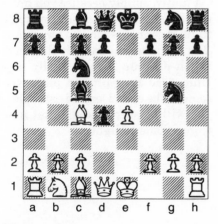

Diagram 30.6

This position was reached after the opening moves:

**1 e4 e5 2 Nf3 Nc6 3 d4 exd4 4 Bc4 Bc5 5 Ng5?** White has moved his Knight twice, starting a premature attack when he should have carried on developing pieces. But Black did not defend very well. He played:

**5 ... Ne5**, which at first glance

doesn't look a bad move. It guards his f-pawn and attacks the Bishop. But it is a bad move because by unnecessarily moving a piece twice Black allows White's plan to succeed.

**6 Nxf7! Nxf7 7 Bxf7+ Kxf7 8 Qh5+ g6 9 Qxc5**, and White has the advantage because he is attacking the d-pawn and Black cannot make any particularly useful moves. See diagram 30.7.

The great Paul Morphy (1837–84) found a much better defensive move from the position shown in diagram 30.6. Can you find it?

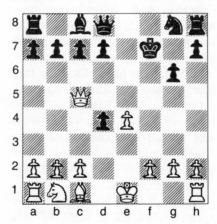

Diagram 30.7

Finally, a very common opening position arises after the following moves:

**1 e4 e5 2 Nf3 Nc6 3 Bc4 Nf6 4 Ng5!?**

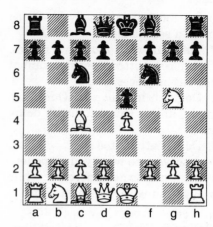

Diagram 30.8

Although this moves a piece twice, opening experts say it is acceptable (remember what we said about exceptions to the 'rules'). In fact, one of the authors of this book – John Littlewood – has won literally hundreds of games in simultaneous displays from this position as White – even though he prefers Black here!

Can you suggest how play might continue for a few moves? Who do *you* think the position favours, Black or White?

Here is a brief summary of the 'rules' governing opening play.

* Develop your pieces in the fewest possible moves to what you consider to be their 'best' squares in that particular opening.

* Use your pieces and pawns together – in harmony – and do not let them get in each other's way.

* Try to develop most of your pieces

before moving an already developed piece a second time.

* Take care with your pawn moves. Once committed pawns cannot retreat as pieces can.

* Do not bring out your Queen too early, unless you can justify doing so.

* Do not attack too soon.

* Always note what your opponent is doing and do not ignore him while you get on with your own plans.

### Solutions

**Diagram 30.1** White wins the exchange by 5 Na4!, when the Rook has three possible moves, all of which lose, as follows:

(a) 5 ... Rb4 6 c3.

(b) 5 ... Rc6 6 Bb5 (Ne5 is also good) Rd6 7 e5 Rd5 8 c4.

(c) 5 ... Rd6 6 e5 Rd5 7 c4 Ra5 8 Bd2 Ra6 9 c5 b5 10 Bxb5 (or cxb6 ep).

In line (c) White wins a Rook for only a pawn if Black plays 7 ... Bb4+, by 8 Bd2 Bxd2 9 Qxd2.

**Diagram 30.5** Botvinnik won by 9 Na4! Qxa2 10 Bc4 Bg4 11 Nf3, and Spielmann resigned after 11 ... Qa3 12 Rc3! and Black has to give up his Knight ( ... Nc2+) in order to save the Queen. If Black played 9 ... Qa3 at once, we have the same idea in a different sequence, 10 Rc3! Qxa2 11 Bc4, etc.

**Diagram 30.6** It is much better to bring out an *extra* piece to defend against the attack on the f-pawn rather than move the same piece twice. Morphy played 5 ... Nh6! when White's intended combination turns out badly for him after Nxf7 Nxf7 7 Bxf7+ Kxf7 8 Qh5+ g6 9 Qxc5. Compare this position with that reached after the 5 ... Ne5? line (diagram 30.7). You will see that after Black plays 9 ... d6, attacking the Queen, White has lost time since Black's pawn on d4 is now defended and 10 Qc4+ Be6 allows Black to gain even more time. An instructive example!

**Diagram 30.8** Black's best move here is 4 ... d5! 5 exd5, and now *not* the risky 5 ... Nd5? (when 6 d4 gives White an excellent game as many players have found to their cost) but one of the following ideas:

(a) 6 ... Na5! 7 Bb5+ c6! 8 dxc6 bxc6 with even chances. If White had played 7 d3 instead of Bb5+, Black would have gained a good position with 7 ... h6 8 Nf3 e4 9 Qe2 Nxc4 10 dxc4 Bc5.

(b) 6 ... b5! 7 Bxb5 Qxd5 8 Nc3 Qxg2 9 Qf3 Qxf3 10 Nxf3 Bd7 with an equal game. After 6 ... b5! 7 Bf1! Nd4! leads to really complicated play, the outcome of which is anybody's guess (or it could be determined by whoever makes the last-but-one mistake!).

If you have studied the last three Units properly, you will appreciate that getting away to a good start is essential in chess.

By all means learn set openings from books which deal with them – if you want to – but you must spend time in trying to find out *why* certain moves are considered best in given situations, and search out the object of each type of opening. Then, whenever your opponent plays moves that are not 'in the book' you will not be thrown out of your stride and left wondering what to do next.

Finally, simply because you have now finished this book you must not think it cannot teach you any more. You will almost certainly find that if you dip into it at virtually any Unit, read it again and play over some of the exercises and examples, you will be surprised at what new things come to light.